Sea, Salt & Sweat

A Story of Nova Scotia and the vast Atlantic Fisheries

Nova Scotia
Department of Fisheries
Halifax, Canada
Crown copyright 1977

Produced by
the
Nova Scotia Communications
and Information Centre, Box 2206, Halifax, N.S. B3J 3C4

ISBN 0-88871-001-1

In the
Realm of
the Ocean Sea

Nova Scotia today is the biggest North American fisherman in the Northwest Atlantic. The leading fishing province of Atlantic Canada, it catches more sea fish than any of the New England States which also border on the famed and fertile crescent of ocean fishing banks that embrace this historic coast.

Ocean fishing is our first and oldest industry, dating back to the early 1500s, and all around Nova Scotia's thousands of miles of briny coastline still perch the steepled towns and painted sea villages that are the home ports of some of the best fishermen in the world.

One of the original provinces of the Canadian confederation, Nova Scotia lies like a leaf-green jewel on the crest of the everlasting Atlantic, just south of the latitude that takes the great River of Canada to meet the ocean depths. With the other Maritime Provinces of New Brunswick and Prince Edward Island, Nova Scotia forms with Newfoundland and Labrador an informal ocean archipelago, enjoying its own distinctive heritage and culture, and called Atlantic Canada.

This part of Canada did not grow up on beaver pelts or wheat or metals, but on the incredible dry salt cod. For centuries the bountiful codfish, inshore and on our fishing banks, was the basic commodity item produced on this northerly coast of North America for international trade.

It was the cod which drew the early fishermen and the first merchants, traders and colonists to these sea-swept shores. Jaunty fishing captains ruled our bays a century before Canada's first successful colonists arrived, and when the American Pilgrims put ashore at Plymouth Rock the fishermen were already there to sell them cod.

Though the fishermen of many nations have worked the international waters off our coast, the Portuguese, French and English, by turns, developed and dominated the early fishery. Soon Newfoundland, New England and Nova Scotia rivalled one another in the industry.

In early trans-Atlantic commerce the salt dry cod produced in these North American colonies was the basic commodity on the rich ocean trading route called the Golden Triangle. Shipped to Spain and the Mediterranean, our cod was exchanged for higher-priced commodities and currency which multiplied the returns to England. This process of trading up the value of commodities was later extended to exchanging cod for West Indian sugar, and built a huge volume of ocean shipping.

While the successful competition of New England in that trade helped provoke the American Revolution, in the next century fisheries diplomacy and the cod had an important political role in bringing Nova Scotia into the Canadian confederation.

In the later days of empire, the salt dry cod enabled emigrating Europeans to survive the tropics, and fed the expanding populations of the cities. The cod's high-protein content and matchless keeping qualities made it a staple at home and abroad. The cod travelled into battle with Europe's ambitious armies and navies, and was tucked into the knapsacks of all those dauntless explorers of jungles and icecaps.

Twentieth century technology replaced the tall ships and schooners with motor-driven trawlers and draggers, and the sails and sweeps of the inshore fleets gave way to gas engines. At the same time the curing process of the salt dry cod was largely overtaken by the demand for fresh and frozen fillets, markets changed and the traditional character of the fisheries was transformed to meet modern needs.

Though the cod is still the backbone of the fishing industry on this coast, Nova Scotia fisheries have become diversified. The inshore fishery undertaken from hundreds of ports around the province, and the offshore fishery conducted by deepsea vessels, are equally important. Scallops and lobsters now bring Nova Scotia fishermen more cash than cod and other groundfish, or the growing herring fishery.

Eventually, massive new fishing technology on the offshore banks threatened the ability of the cod and other groundfish to survive. Efforts to prevent over-fishing and further depletion of the fish stocks by foreign fleets in the Northwest Atlantic, led to Canada's declaration in January 1977 of a 200-mile fisheries limit.

Primarily a conservation measure to prevent the possible extinction of fisheries resources on this coast, the declaration also provided the opportunity for gradual redevelopment of the Canadian fisheries industry to match the changing conditions of world demand.

In order to harvest its share of the fish stocks as they are built up under Canadian scientific management over the next decade, the fishing industry will require new fleets, including sophisticated freezer trawlers, and new markets overseas. The planning is already underway, and by 1980 Nova Scotia alone expects to double its present catch of sea fish.

In recognition of the great importance of the sea fisheries to these provinces and states by the ocean, the cod has been memorialized inventively over the centuries: a cod was engraved on early Nova Scotia banknotes with the hopeful motto, ''success to the fisheries;'' while Massachusetts' ''sacred'' carved-pine cod has hung in the state house since the revolution.

However, the most inspiring symbol of the Northwest Atlantic fisheries, and the hearty Nova Scotia men who followed the calling, was *Bluenose* — the fastest deep sea fishing schooner of them all. Today the Government of Nova Scotia operates a full-size replica of *Bluenose* to help tell the Nova Scotia story.

The navigator John Cabot's little ship Mathew in which he discovered the northern approaches to the New World and first found the abundance of cod in the Northwest Atlantic.

When Cod was King

It was the discovery of the new lands on what is now the Canadian Atlantic coast, by John Cabot in the summer of 1497, that started the great Northwest Atlantic fisheries. When the little ship *Mathew* returned to Bristol after nearly three months at sea, Cabot and his companions, nearly all English and from Bristol, were feted in the streets of the seaport town. Lorenzo Pasqualigo wrote his brothers in Venice that vast honour was paid to Cabot. "He is called the Great Admiral . . . and these English run after him like mad."

They were celebrating Cabot's discovery of the new lands overseas, and not the codfish, not yet. In fact the English would need another century to begin exploiting this fishery on a large scale. However, King Henry VII was pleased. He gave a small annuity and made a token gift of " £10 to hym that founde the new Isle." He also promised a fleet of ships for the disastrous voyage of 1498, from which the Great Admiral never returned.

The English had been fishing and trading in Iceland since the 12th century, and Bristol merchants from the early 1400s had shipped their Iceland stockfish — a hard dried cod — to the ports of Spain and Portugal, trading for wine and oil for sale in Britain, Iceland and the continent. Beginning in 1480 Bristol merchants sent numerous unsuccessful voyages into the Atlantic seeking islands west of Ireland with fishing or other commercial potential. From 1490 until Cabot arrived in 1495, they were sending two to four ships a year in search of the islands popularized in the medieval epic about the Irish voyager, St. Brendan.

Cabot and his Bristol crew had dutifully reported the abundance of cod found on their first voyage in the coastal waters of the new lands. The Venetian also made maps, and both the information on the fishery and the maps showing the location of the new lands, were soon circulated throughout maritime Europe. In a letter to the Duke of Milan, Raimondo de Soncino wrote: "They assert that the sea there is swarming with fish, which can be taken not only with the net, but in baskets let down with a stone, so that it sinks in the water. I have heard this Messer Zoane (John) state so much. These same English, his companions, say that they could bring so many fish that this kingdom would have no further need of Iceland, from which place there comes a very great quantity of the fish called stockfish."

However, the English did not exploit the new overseas fishery immediately. It was more distant and at the time more hazardous than the Iceland fishery, required different curing, and may have conflicted with established English interests in Iceland. In any case, it was not the English but the French and Portuguese who initiated and developed the fishery in the new lands during the early 1500s.

Portuguese interest in the new lands sent their crisp caravels exploring north from the Azores in 1500. Joao Fernandes, a former trader in Bristol, reached Greenland and named it Lavrador for his position as *lavrador* or landholder at home — a name later transferred to the present Labrador. The following year Gaspar Corte-Real and his brother Miguel made the east coast of what is now Newfoundland, and explored from Bonavista to Cape Race. Both Corte-Reals were lost at sea within a year, but first they found a fragment of Venetian sword among the Indians indicating that Cabot probably made that same coast on his fateful 1498 voyage.

Despite the increasing number of voyages to the new lands in the early 1500s, geographical information remained slight, and often confused. The English designation "New Lands" or "New Found Lands" was not exclusive to the

A Portuguese caravel in the period of North American discovery.

present island of Newfoundland, but covered the whole of the known coast, including southern Labrador, the east coast of Newfoundland, and Cape Breton Island in northern Nova Scotia. The Portuguese name, Corte-Real Land, or *Bacallaos* meaning codfish land, included the Bonavista-Cape Race coast. The French name *Terre-Neuves* covered the same territory as the English. Only gradually did the names and locations become more specific.

Scholars remain divided on whether Cabot's *Mathew* actually landed in Cape Breton or on the east coast of Newfoundland. Both Canadian provinces claim the historic Cabot landing. Cape Breton is one of the oldest European place names in North American geography. And if it was not discovered and named by John Cabot, it was located soon afterwards by the Bretons and Normans. The *Discorso* of historian Giovanni Ramusio written in 1539 notes that the part of Terra Nova running east and west was discovered 35 years ago (1504) by the Brettoni and Normandi, for which reason that land is called il capo delli Brettoni.

The fishing industry of the Northwest Atlantic probably began in that year of 1504, with the fishing ships of Portugal and of Brittany and Normandy arriving in the coastal waters of the new lands about the same time. The Portuguese fished along the Bonavista-Cape Race coast of Bacallaos which they believed to be an island; and the Bretons and Normans along "that part of Terra Nova running east and west," embracing part of the south coast of Newfoundland and Cape Breton Island, and the coast north of Bonavista.

It was the Portuguese who attempted the first colony in the new land. Joao Fagundez of the Portuguese fishing capital of Viana, advocated the colony as a base for curing and shipping fish, thus saving the long voyage home to

A 13th century English fishing vessel of the style used in the Iceland trade.

Viana and Lisbon made by every Portuguese fishing ship. In 1520 he explored the south coast of Newfoundland, St. Pierre, and Cape Breton Island which he called St. John. The following year he returned with Portuguese fishermen and their families from Viana and the Azores and established his settlement in Cape Breton, probably at Ingonish. However, conflict with the Micmac Indians and with Breton fishermen in the area soon destroyed the Portuguese colony.

Exact destinations of the European fishermen in the new lands are hard to find. Fishermen usually kept such information to themselves for reasons of competition — and still do. We know the French Basque fisherman Savalet was fishing in 1563 at Whitehaven, south of Canso, only because Marc Lescarbot who interviewed him there in 1606 relates the tale. The reports of visiting captains and early business archives reveal something of the numbers of ships and men involved, but little or nothing of their ports in this country, or their personal lives, only an occasional name.

Early Portuguese and French place names in Nova Scotia, as in Newfoundland, usually indicated the presence of fishermen, as well as occasional explorers. Portuguese names from the first half of the 1500s include: Mira, Gabarus, Baccaro, possibly Canso, and Bras d'Or — from Lavrador, Fernandes' name for Greenland, once associated with Cape Breton. Hybrid Portuguese and French names on various 16th century charts indicated the early presence of French fishermen as well as Portuguese.

Louisbourg Harbour, site of the famed 18th century French fortress, was English Harbour in the 17th century and the Portuguese Bretois before that. Sydney Harbour, formerly Spanish Bay, was previously Ribeiro de Sam Pablo, while the Portuguese originally named Cape Smoky,

A dogger boat used by French and English in the early fisheries.

12

A European fishing ship of the early 16th century taking cod in the New Land.
(From an early print)

near Ingonish, Fudos or Fumos — meaning smokes. Both Isle Madame and St. Peters are counterparts of early Portuguese names. Baia di Isles was a hybrid name for the island-strewn eastern shore of Nova Scotia, from Beaver Harbour to Marie Joseph. Another Portuguese-French hybrid was Ribeira de Jardines, meaning River of Gardens, later called Passapec by the French and, later still, Prospect by the English. This early fishing centre, near Halifax, likely got its hybrid name from the vegetable gardens or jardines normally planted by the fishing masters. Jordan River near Shelburne probably received its name in the same way. Le Beau Baia was the present Port Joli, and Beu Sablon, meaning Bay of Sand, referred to the waters adjacent to Cape Sable. The numerous early French place names — many based on Micmac Indian words — appeared with later French cartography.

Place names from the maps of the 1500s, however, reflect something of the extent of the fishery and the distribution of European fishermen: Bretons, Normans, Portuguese, Basques, followed by the Spanish and English, all along the Atlantic coast of Nova Scotia, from Cape Breton Island to the Bay of Fundy.

In the beginning it was the Breton pilots and seamen who furnished the skills, while merchants of the French channel ports, Rouen and Dieppe, and later those of La Rochelle, Bayonne, Bordeaux and St. Jean de Luz, provided the financing, management and marketing organization. Besides the technical ability and the shipping, France had abundant supplies of solar salt for curing the cod to French tastes. Some 14 million people — more than three times the population of England — meant a strong demand for the fish at home. This domestic market, served by ports dispersed around the French coast from Calais to the

Pyrenees, provided the vital basis for overseas fisheries. As early as 1532 growth of the French fishing industry helped propel the old duchy of Brittany into union. Italian banking houses moved into the fishing centres with new capital resources, while the French developed and dominated the fishing during most of the 16th century.

Four hundred years ago, this year, the European fishing fleets on the coasts of Newfoundland, Cape Breton and southern Labrador, totalled 315 ships of some 60 to 200 tons, and about 6,000 men. They came from France, Portugal, Spain — and England, which accounted for the 15. But new developments were already underway. The Spanish fishing fleet had been building up since the middle of the century to become one of the largest in the New World, while the Portuguese in their noble barkes were about to vanish with the union of Portugal and Spain in 1581 — until the arrival on the banks of the romantic Portuguese white fleet in the early 20th century. With the destruction of the Spanish Armada in 1588, the Spanish fishing fleet also declined rapidly, not to return until modern times. This soon left the whole of the rich Iberian market open to the French and English export competition.

In France the Northwest Atlantic cod fishery was already big business, and highly specialized. Much of the industry was organized to produce large "green" or "wet" salted cod, brought home in the holds of the fishing ships, and barreled up "wet" for metropolitan Paris and French regional markets. It was to better supply the high-priced market for "wet" cured fish that some of the French fishing ships before 1550 began moving, from the bays and harbours where the fishery started, to fishing grounds 100 miles or more offshore, on the famed Newfoundland and Nova Scotia fishing banks.

An early cod fisherman dressed in oiled skins, baits up. (Based on an old print)

A smaller proportion of the French industry produced "dry" salted cod. The Bretons and the French Basques from ports in the Bay of Biscay produced "dry" cured fish for French and export markets. Neither the French dry-cured cod fishery nor, of course, the "wet" fish industry, required much in the way of shore facilities in the new lands. The French had plenty of solar salt from salt pans at home, and the dry curing of overseas fish was carried out on the beaches of Biscay and the French channel ports. While the Basques had extended their Biscay whale hunting to the new lands in the 16th century, and took walrus, all the extensive French fisheries and related enterprises were relatively self-sufficient and, in the 1500s, did little to support settlement in the new lands.

English conditions were quite different. Dependence on stockfish from Iceland restrained English fishermen, particularly those from the English east coast ports, from entering the Northwest Atlantic fishery. A few English fishing vessels were in the new lands as early as 1522, when the navy provided a wartime escort for the "commyng home of the New founde Isle flete." In the second half of the century, however, the fishing industry began shifting concentration from the English east coast to ports in the West of England — those along the English Channel, such as Southampton, Plymouth and Falmouth — and also Bristol on the southwest coast. These and other West Country ports developed the English fishery in the new lands.

The lack of solar salt had been the technical deterrent to early growth of the English fishery overseas. The wet salted and even the heavily salted dry cures of the French required vast supplies of solar salt. Before the discovery of mineral salt, the Portuguese and Spanish, as well as the French, operated huge salt pans, producing salt from the evaporation of sea water by the heat of the sun. England did not have the climate for it, and salt imports were costly. The English experience with hard air-dried stockfish from Iceland, coupled with rising market demands for dry salt cod, eventually produced an English cure using minimum salt which was adaptable to fishing in the new lands.

Since the beginning of the middle ages the sea fishing nations of Europe traded internationally, and the fishing industry was the first in Europe to be organized on an international scale. From the eighth century, when the church began to allow fish for meals on fast days, production and marketing was scheduled to the weekly fast days and the demands of the Lenten season. A large portion of this established demand was traditionally supplied with Swedish herring. When north European resources of herring in the mid-16th century unaccountably disappeared for some years, much of that European market turned to cod, increasing demand as well as prices.

At the same time the English were taking official measures to try and boost English overseas fishing efforts, in the face of rising imports from such countries as France. From 1541 Henry VIII fined the importers, and to help increase the domestic market, Queen Elizabeth later added an extra fast day to the week. However, no government measure seemed so effective in moving English fishermen into the Northwest Atlantic as the Danish decision in 1580 to levy license fees on foreign fishing in Iceland.

Colonies
of the
Golden Triangle

In 1583 the boisterous Elizabethan courtier Sir Humphrey Gilbert had sailed into St. John's harbour in Newfoundland and officially taken the entire island for the English crown, threatening captains of the international fishing fleet who were present, that any who spoke ill of his queen would lose both their ships and their ears. Gilbert's grand gesture was based on English claims originating with the discoveries of John Cabot. His commission allowed him practically anything he could take between Labrador and Florida, and his intention was to found a colony in what is now New England, but he never saw the Norumbega territory. He went down with his ship on the way home from Sable Island, and was said to be reading at the time from Sir Thomas More's *Utopia*.

The West Country English fishing fleet built up quickly, first on the Atlantic coast of the Avalon peninsula, which had been dominated by the Portuguese. The English bought their salt on the fishing grounds from the Portuguese, and made their lightly-salted dry cod at shore-based fishing establishments in the coves and harbours of the new land. In the early years, the fishing ships carried their own dry cured fish back to England for transport by London merchant ships to the growing Spanish and Mediterranean export markets. Out of this arrangement grew the fabulous golden triangle which built up and dominated ocean trade in the north and south Atlantic for two centuries.

The presence of the expanding and aggressive English fishery forced the French to the south coast of Newfoundland, the offshore fishing banks, the Gulf, and, particularly, more and more into Cape Breton and what is now mainland Nova Scotia. Extension of the competitive English and French fishing efforts, from one fishing trip a year to two and three, tended to require more permanent facilities in the

An early North American fishing base with stages for sun-drying the cod, sheds for splitting and salting, and one of the knockdown boats brought along for shore fishing. (From an early print)

new lands. The first trips of the year were most profitable, and English fishermen in the 17th century began wintering at English Harbour (Louisbourg) in Cape Breton, to make the fishing grounds in January. By the end of the century an estimated 500 ships of all nations worked the Northwest Atlantic fisheries, including some 200 at Cape Breton and the Nova Scotia shore.

Nicholas Denys, one of the French colonial pioneers in Nova Scotia during the 1600s, reported that on a summer voyage he made around the entire coast of the old province, from the Penobscot River in what is now Maine, around the Atlantic coast of Nova Scotia, including Cape Breton, and the Gulf coast to the Gaspe, he found numerous fishing ships and their boats in nearly every harbour of any size.

While Nova Scotia was occupied largely by the French, who called the land *Acadie,* the English fishery spread from Newfoundland southwest of Nova Scotia, along the coast of what is now New England, as far as Cape Cod. In 1602 Bartholemew Gosnold named the cape for the multitudes of fish which ''vexed'' his ship, and John Smith by 1614 was the moving spirit behind English fishing establishments at Monhegan and in the Pemaquid region of Maine. It was Captain Smith who vigorously pointed out to his English colleagues that fish might be a mere commodity of trade, but would become a greater source of treasure than all the colonial gold and silver mines of Spain. Of course, he was right.

The first French colonial attempt came in 1598 with the expedition of a colorful marquis named Troilus de La Roche de Mesgouez. Enthused by the profits of the French fishery which he saw at St. Malo, de La Roche got a commission from the French crown as early as 1577 — the year before Gilbert obtained his patent from Queen Elizabeth — to undertake a plantation in the Terres-Neuves. Civil wars and imprisonment kept the marquis from his task until 1597 when he was appointed the first viceroy in New France, and the following year established on Nova Scotia's Sable Island. Many of his ''settlers'' were ex-prisoners from French jails; nevertheless, La Roche conducted successful fisheries and trading operations from the island until 1604 when the failure of supply ships caused such hardships the colonists were returned to France.

Legends of earlier French colonial efforts on this coast persist, but the historical data is slight. Sable Island, on one of the largest Nova Scotia fishing banks, was a fishing base from the early 1500s. The Portuguese and possibly others left cattle there as early as 1550 for the use of the fishing fleets, and there may have been casual efforts to settle before La Roche.

Notable among the legendary attempts at settlement connected with the fisheries is the one possibly made at Canso around 1529. Marc Lescarbot offered the first tip in his 1609 history of New France, citing a Baron de Lery undertaking to settle in Nova Scotia at that time but finding that for lack of feed he had to put his cattle ashore on Sable. Canso was a fishing base from the earliest times, but scholars have been unable to trace any record of the grant, or indeed of the baron. However, this too may have been a casual settlement intended to serve the early fisheries, and unrecorded in colonial files.

Port Royal was the first permanent settlement by Europeans on this continent north of the Gulf of Mexico. Now Annapolis Royal, on a long basin of the sea extending to the Bay of Fundy, it was founded in the summer of 1605 by the French trader Pierre Du Gua de Monts and his famed French navigator Samuel de Champlain. Port Royal was the first of a series of relatively successful colonial ventures by French and English in the first quarter of the 17th century, from the Chesapeake to the St. Lawrence and Conception Bay. In 1607 the English established Jamestown in Virginia, after a couple of failures to settle at Roanoake in the 1580s under Sir Walter Raleigh. Champlain established Quebec in 1608. Though St. John's was "populous" with visiting fishermen and run by the fishing admirals when Gilbert arrived there in 1583, the first official colony in Newfoundland was Sir John Guy's short-lived settlement in 1610 at Cuper's Cove, now Cupids on Conception Bay. In 1620 the Pilgrim fathers arrived to begin colonizing New England.

The success of the French and English fisheries was a strong factor in promoting the new colonies, though the new settlements were not directly related to fisheries' interests. In what is now Atlantic Canada and New England, the powerful English fishing interests tended to discourage settlement in Newfoundland while supporting it in New England. In Nova Scotia during the French regime, colonial interests, initially concerned with fur trading, worked out an intermittent accord.

Essentially, the fisheries were based on notions of free trade, aggressive commercialism and competition, and were controlled by the rising merchant class in both nations. Colonial settlement, on the other hand, imposed traditional forms of land grants and tenure, involving overlords and tenants, wide-ranging property rights and fealties, licensing and trade monopolies. The two systems were in conflict.

In New England the problem was eased by early development of a sedentary or resident fishery conducted by the settlers, and the fact that many of them were dissident middle class themselves. Moreover, Massachusetts was

A 17th century colonial ketch from which the famed schooners of this coast derived.

nearly a thousand miles farther than Newfoundland from England. And Governor Edward Winslow took as much pride in the fishery as John Smith.

In Newfoundland the rights of the fishermen to use the shoreline for taking fish seemed entrenched, and the powerful English fishery resisted any encroachment by colonial landowners. At Ferryland, Sir David Kirke, the first governor, was called to account for his interference with the fisheries. At one time building anywhere near the shore was prohibited. Such anti-colonial practices eventually drove many fishermen-settlers to the tiny isolated outports around the Newfoundland coast.

In Nova Scotia Charles La Tour was respectful towards the French fisheries on the coasts of *Acadie* or Acadia. His personal establishment near Cape Sable on the present site of Port La Tour was closely related to the fisheries. So was his later settlement across the Bay of Fundy at Saint John. Settlers in the seigneury he granted Phillipe Mius d'Entremont in 1651 began a resident sea fishery at Pubnico Harbour which has flourished in the Pubnicos to this day.

Isaac de Razilly, the French naval commander who shared control of Acadia with La Tour, arrived in 1632 at La Have and tried to build up the fisheries. He fortified the important fishing port of Canso and, with Nicholas Denys, built a resident sea fishery at Port Rossignol, now Liverpool. Razilly brought out salt makers to develop salt pans on the tidal marshes at Port Royal. The settlers he introduced from France were the first of the famed Acadians whose dykelands and farms by the end of the century stretched from Port Royal and Petite Riviere to the Gulf of St. Lawrence. While La Tour and Razilly's successor, Charles de Menou D'Aulnay, fought each other in colorful baronial wars, Denys energetically set up fishing and trading centres in half a dozen locations throughout Acadia: St. Peters and St. Ann's in Cape Breton, Chedabucto near Canso, and Miscou, Nipisiguit and possibly the Miramichi on the gulf coast of New Brunswick. By 1698 the Sedentary Fishing Company of Acadia began short-lived operations on what is now Halifax harbour.

But the conflicts between overlapping French monopolies within Acadia, and the difficulties of trying to prohibit or else license the competitive fishermen and traders arriving on this coast from New England, worked against the development of successful sedentary or resident fisheries. As a business venture, two of La Tour's sons-in-law undertook licensing New England vessels to fish on the coast. French fishermen objected. The commandant of Acadia, Michel Leneuf, sieur de La Vallière, also encouraged the New Englanders to fish and trade by license in Acadia, and in 1683 was fired for his enterprise.

Jacques-Francois de Brouillan, one of the last French governors of Acadia, wrote the court that fishing might still become the country's principal industry though it had been ruined by many years of war and privateering. He proposed to train more Acadians for sea fishing. Frustrated by the advance of the New England fishing fleets, however, Brouillan turned La Have into a pirate lair and sent his buccaneers to destroy New England fishing vessels and merchantmen.

From 1670 on, the New Englanders had operated as many as 30 shallops out of Liverpool harbour, and some 15 large vessels from La Have. Salem and Marblehead fishermen in 1699 offered to pay fees for permission to fish the Nova Scotia Banks; and by 1708 an estimated 300 New England fishing vessels were on this coast. The trading monopolies which served Quebec well in the fur-trading interior of the continent did not work in the commercial fisheries. In French Acadia the problem was not resolved but superseded by more than a century of wars, sieges, raids and rampant piracy, which made the province a battleground for contending imperial trade and territorial ambitions.

The first proud settlement of Port Royal, established by Champlain and DeMonts in 1605, had been captured in 1613 by Samuel Argall of Virginia, leaving the inhabitants to take shelter with the Micmac Indians. It was Champlain who called the country *Acadie* or Acadia from the name Arcadia given by the 16th century explorer Verrazzano to a portion of the coast. The Scottish courtier Sir William Alexander in 1621 named it Nova Scotia, which was Jacobean Latin for New Scotland. Baronetcies of Nova Scotia were introduced by the king to encourage support for Alexander's ambitious plans to colonize the entire region. However, his British settlement near the site of Port Royal was captured by Razilly in 1632, after less than three years, and another at Baleine in a matter of months. From the time Port Royal was founded until its final capture by the English in 1710, this former colonial capital changed hands between the super powers of the day seven times.

By this time the expanding fishing and trading enterprises of New England were already threatening English prosperity at home. The rich triangular Atlantic trade initiated by the fishing companies of the West Country and based on the dry salt cod, had helped build a huge English merchant fleet. While the Northwest Atlantic fisheries were considered as the "nursery of the British navy," the navigation acts of the 17th century, requiring all goods to be shipped in English bottoms, protected and enhanced both shipping and trade.

— Shallop —
A handliner of 1770

Dry salt cod was the primary commodity in the Atlantic export triangle, and as trade grew the system became more sophisticated. It had started with West Country ships fishing and carrying their cod directly to Spanish and Mediterranean markets, trading it for higher priced commodities and for Spanish currency, returning the higher value items to England, then picking up supplies and heading back to the fishing grounds. Vessels called sack ships improved the system but reduced the function of the big English fishing ships. The sack ships supplied the sedentary fisheries in New England and Newfoundland, bought their fish and carried it to the same markets. The French in Nova Scotia and in Placentia, Newfoundland, could not compete but the other English — those in New England, could.

With a couple of amendments, the New Englanders got around the stringent English navigation code, fished and traded freely with Europe, duplicating the triangle run but with the profits to New England instead of the Old Country. With the development of sugar plantations in the West Indies in the mid-17th century New England became the key supplier, trading its salt fish, plus timber and farm products, for West Indian sugar to sell in England and the continent. Again the French fishery could not do a similar job. Their empire of the St. Lawrence, based on the fur trade, was too remote and could not be co-ordinated with Acadia or Placentia to supply the plantations of the French West Indies. So, indirectly, the New Englanders also supplied the French islands. All this led to expansion of the New England fisheries to encompass Nova Scotia.

The loss by the French of all Acadia, except Cape Breton Island, to the English by treaty in 1713, coincided with the loss of their Newfoundland fishing base at Placentia. Retaining fishing privileges along the "French" shore of

Newfoundland, French fishing interests moved to Cape Breton and were concentrated in Louisbourg. Louis XIV ordered construction of the mightiest fortress in the new world to protect the sun king's beleaguered North American empire. In its brief life-span, Louisbourg became a cosmopolitan seaport, redolent of trade and intrigue. But it could no more co-ordinate French colonial trade in the Atlantic than Placentia. New England traders helped support Louisbourg as a profitable market until the fortress became a threat. In 1745, a rag-tag army of New England farmers and fishermen captured it and, though the English traded it back to France in 1748 (to be taken again a decade later), they sent Colonel Edward Cornwallis the following year to found Halifax and fortify it as a guardian of the North Atlantic.

In and around Nova Scotia the New Englanders had introduced a new method of fishing. French government officials noticed it as early as 1699. Using smart little two-masted ketches of 20 to 40 tons, crewed by as few as five men, they in effect extended shore fishing operations for dry salt cod to the offshore Nova Scotia Banks. In their ketches, the New Englanders took cod on the banks, salting it down wet in the holds until they came ashore where the fish was immediately washed, sun-dried and cured on any beach available. The ketches were faster and more efficient in the dry fish trade than the big French and English fishing ships. Being close to base, the small vessels fished day and night, summer and winter. They would also make a couple of winter voyages carrying their cod to the West Indies when return cargoes of sugar were available. Such vessels were the forerunners of the great saltbankers and the Nova Scotia schooner trade.

As the small fore-and-aft rigged schooners, of 50 tons or

Handlining from the deck of a schooner on the offshore banks in the 19th century. (After an old print)

more, evolved from the ketch in the early 18th century, the New England fishermen were able to occupy the Nova Scotia Banks more extensively. With southwest winds prevailing along this coast the schooner was an ideal sailing craft. Manned by a crew of seven, it could handle winter icing comfortably since nobody had to go aloft to set sail as in the square-rigged vessels. With these small efficient schooners, Canso became an important centre in the dry fishery. They fished the banks from March through December, beginning with Sable Island Bank, then Browns, Georges, and back to Sable for winter cod.

As soon as Canso was surrendered by the French in 1713, the English in Nova Scotia and from New England moved in to control the fisheries. English sack ships supplied Canso and delivered its fish to Spain and the Mediterranean markets. As early as 1724 the annual New England trade in cod through Canso totalled £150 thousand, and Lawrence Armstrong, the Lieutenant-Governor of Nova Scotia, urged that the colonial capital be moved there from Annapolis Royal. However, the competition of Louisbourg and raids by the French restrained development, and when the New Englanders captured the fortress in 1745, Canso was the port from which they sailed.

Though political control of Nova Scotia passed to the new colonial capital of Halifax in 1749, the population remained mostly Acadian, or neutral French as they were called, while the fishing economy of the country was very much in the hands of New England interests. Efforts to draw immigration from Europe brought some 3,000 settlers from the German and French states of the old Holy Roman Empire, Switzerland and Holland, to Halifax in 1750-52. Mostly German-speaking, in 1753 they founded Lunenburg which later became Nova Scotia's leading offshore fishing

Fishing vessels handlining on the banks in the 1830s.
(Based on old prints)

port — home of the heroic banks fishermen and their tall schooners like *Bluenose*.

Continuing conflict between the French and English in 1755 forced the tragic expulsion of the Acadians from Nova Scotia. Three years later the English took Louisbourg again and this time blew it to bits. The capture of Quebec the following year put an end to French military power in North America. And by 1760 the arrival of New England settlers began in southwestern Nova Scotia. Many were fishermen who already knew this coast well.

The New Englanders had been fishing since at least 1670 from the Liverpool area of Nova Scotia and in 1760 they came to stay. Over half of the settlers, from Connecticut, were fishermen and they brought over a dozen schooners with them, which left immediately for the Nova Scotia Banks. Simeon Perkins, merchant and diarist of Liverpool, whose historic house still stands in the town, sent his schooners to fish cod for markets in Europe and the West Indies. He noted in 1767 that his schooners *Polly* and the *Jolly Fisherman* worked a new bank, probably Hamilton Inlet Bank, off Labrador, and fished the Grand Bank and off Scatari.

Fishermen from Nantucket, Cape Cod and Plymouth, began settling in the Barrington-Cape Sable area in 1761, and the same year the first fishing families from New England arrived in Yarmouth. After the loss of Cape Breton by the French, fishing firms from the Channel Islands of Jersey and Guernsey established in Arichat on Isle Madame, to help serve French markets. Acadians, back from their lengthy exile, turned to Isle Madame and the Cheticamp area of Cape Breton, to work in those fisheries. Their former farm lands elsewhere in the colony occupied by new settlers, other Acadians by 1767 began establishing fisheries in the Meteghan area of western Nova Scotia, as well as returning to Pubnico.

A Chebacco boat or large shallop introduced in the Nova Scotia fisheries in the early 1800s largely by the Loyalists.

Salt Fish and Democracy

With the pressures of the French military and economic presence in North America removed after 1763, the attempts of Britain to restrain and regulate the aggressive commercial competition of the American colonies brought on the Revolutionary War and the loss of Britain's first empire. Halifax's strong ties with London, the relatively remote location of the colony, and the shortage of American naval power, helped prevent Nova Scotia from joining the rebels. Three-quarters of the population was from New England and many were sympathetic to the American cause. At the start of the war whole communities vainly sought neutrality. Fishing schooners ran contraband goods, refugees and escaped prisoners. But the continued attacks of American privateers on the coastal towns and villages, gradually hardened anti-American opinion. Seaports like Liverpool built their own privateers to send against the Americans. Out of the war diverse communities of settlers in the colony found a new unity and identity as Nova Scotians. They also gained new population, as thousands of American loyalists after the revolution were resettled here, founding Sydney, Shelburne, Digby and numerous rural and coastal communities. Cape Cod whalers established in Dartmouth and following the loyalists came Scottish immigrations into Pictou, Antigonish and Cape Breton Island.

With the former American colonies out of the empire, Nova Scotians vigorously sought the trading advantages apparently vacated by New England, both overseas and in the British West Indies. They also sought a better deal in the fisheries than the Treaty of Versailles allowed. After the revolution American fishermen were given freedom to fish any of our coastal waters and cure fish anywhere along unsettled areas of the coast. For the first time, a three-mile limit was firmly established by the historic convention of 1818, restricting Americans to fishing outside the three-mile zone, and entering it only for shelter, repairs and supplies of wood and water.

Meanwhile, as early as 1804 a committee of Halifax merchants took Nova Scotia's case for easing the crippling British navigation laws, to London. That committee was the forerunner of the Halifax Board of Trade and the Canadian Chamber of Commerce. Halifax commercial and political interests saw the protection won for our inshore fishery as a strong basis for building commerce and industry, and negotiating favourable United States tariffs.

Eventually, Britain reversed its restrictive colonial shipping policies, leaving Nova Scotia free to build and man its own ships, and trade anywhere in the world. The journals of the Nova Scotia House of Assembly in 1829 observed that, "For the first time in the history of British North America, its navigation participates in the conveyance of foreign produce to its ultimate destination. Formerly the circuitous voyages, now very advantageously pursued, could not be attempted."

Nova Scotia's fisheries and markets expanded, so did its world trade. In the next half-century the Nova Scotians built and manned one of the world's largest merchant fleets. Trim Nova Scotia windjammers were known in all the principal ports of the globe. But world markets for fish were changing. While the Nova Scotians extended their fish trade into the Mediterranean, European and West Indian markets diminished. The Reciprocity Treaty of 1854 with the United States looked like an answer. It opened the U.S. market duty-free to fish from Nova Scotia and the other British American colonies. Included, of course, was the provision that fishermen from both countries have equal rights to all sea fisheries north of New Jersey, which included the whole of the Northwest Atlantic.

Essentially, the fisheries provisions of the treaty were to ease the problem of New England's temporary domination of the fishing grounds and invasion of territorial waters with expensive and superior fleets of schooners. In a sense, the conflict was a 19th century forerunner of current difficulties with overwhelming offshore fishing technology. Joseph Howe, the Nova Scotia patriot who introduced responsible democratic government in the 1840s, was assigned by London to help make the treaty work for Nova Scotia fishermen. As an imperial fisheries commissioner, however, he had little influence on policy.

Nova Scotia was increasingly frustrated in efforts to persuade the other fishing colonies of the Maritimes, Newfoundland and Quebec, to adopt a common approach on fisheries. The Nova Scotians needed more power to affect international decisions on fisheries and trade than the small seaboard colony had been able to muster by itself. A federal jurisdiction seemed to be the answer. The year after reciprocity ended, Nova Scotia in 1867 became a founding member of the new Canadian nation.

The Nova Scotia fishing industry peaked in the 1880s, inshore and offshore, employing some 30,000 fishermen. Reciprocal fishing and trading arrangements had been resumed in the 1870s with more advantages to Nova Scotia and the other Canadian fishing provinces. Recognizing, in the Treaty of Washington, differences in the value of the coastal fisheries of each nation, one to the other, the Americans made the Halifax Award of $4,500,000 to Canada. It formed the basis of a shipbuilding subsidy which helped produce Nova Scotia's growing schooner fleets.

Nova Scotia schooners such as those of Simeon Perkins

L.B.JENSON

A Clipper Schooner

—1867—

had been working the fishing banks since the 18th century, handlining cod from the deck, anywhere from LaHave and 'Quereau to Labrador and the Grand Banks. In 1852 some 27 schooners were sailing from Lunenburg County ports for the summer codfishery on the banks and the Labrador. By the turn of the century Lunenburg each year sent more than 150 schooners to the banks, and was building annually more vessels than any other port in Canada.

Introduction of the bultow by the French in the 19th century, made the codfishing saltbank schooners much more efficient than the traditional handlining vessels. The bultow or trawl system used a groundline over a mile long set with thousands of baited hooks. On the banks these trawl lines were buoyed, anchored out and tended by ship's boats which were soon succeeded on the schooners by the famed fisherman's dory. Derived from styles of inshore craft, the simple seaworthy two-man dories nested flat on deck and launched quickly. W. N. Zwicker's *Union* in 1871 was the first Lunenburg schooner to use this technique of banks fishing.

While the large schooners of 100 tons or more from Lunenburg, Yarmouth, Digby, Richmond and Shelburne counties took cod, haddock and halibut for the salt fish trade, winter haddock schooners braved the banks for fresh fish, and the smaller schooners of Digby, Yarmouth and Shelburne dropped their dories in flying sets on the nearer banks to race home with iced fresh fish in time for market. But the change in technology away from wood and wind was evident soon after the turn of the century, in the shape and sound of the motor-driven Cape Island boat inshore, and offshore the steam trawlers. The proud schooners of Nova Scotia, with the aid of auxiliary power, miraculously would hold their own until mid-century, but eventually would have to give way to the modern deep sea trawlers.

A Nova Scotian Pinky Schooner
— 1875 —

Tall Spars and Dorymen

The great white-winged fishing schooners of Nova Scotia were among the most beautiful vessels in the world. It is said that when the fleets of schooners, with flying jibs and topsails drawing, sailed from Lunenburg for the offshore grounds, they were like a flight of magnificent birds. Our two-masted fore-and-aft rigged schooners were derived from the 17th century colonial ketch, and were ideal sailing vessels in the prevailing westerly winds of this coast. While the inshore Tancook Whaler evolved from the shallops and Chebacco boats, our offshore vessels, like those of New England, went through many variations, from the clipper and pinky schooner to the knockabout, the Nova Scotia fisherman's schooner and the spoon-bowed elegance of *Bluenose*. The average 100-ton saltbanker carried up to a dozen two-man dories and a crew of 15 to 26. Some schooners carried one-man dories. However, dory fishing on the banks was hazardous. Many men were lost in the storms and fogs shrouding the banks. Finally, in the 1930s, the sailing vessels gave way to fully-powered motor schooners which carried dorymen to the banks as late as 1962. One of these, the *Theresa Connor,* today forms part of Lunenburg Fisheries Museum.

The Knockabout Schooner

A Tancook Schooner

A Tancook Whaler

NOVA SCOTIAN DEEP SEA FISHING SCHOONER

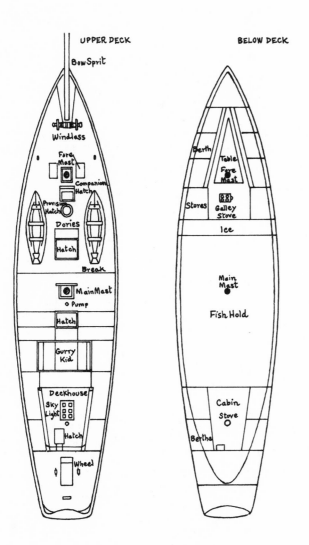

UPPER DECK   BELOW DECK

BowSprit

Windlass

Fore Mast

Companion Hatch

Provision Hatch

Dories

Hatch

Break

MainMast

Pump

Hatch

Gurry Kid

Deckhouse

Sky Light

Hatch

Wheel

Berth

Table

Fore Mast

Stores

Galley Stove

Ice

Main Mast

Fish Hold

Cabin Stove

Berths

The Nova Scotia deep sea fisherman's schooner, the famed saltbanker of the early part of this century. Averaging 95 to 100 tons and 100 feet overall length, these fast and weatherly banks schooners carried up to 8,500 square feet of sail and their main topmasts rose 115 feet above the deck.

The Nova Scotian

DORY

Scale in feet

0 1 2 3 4 5 6

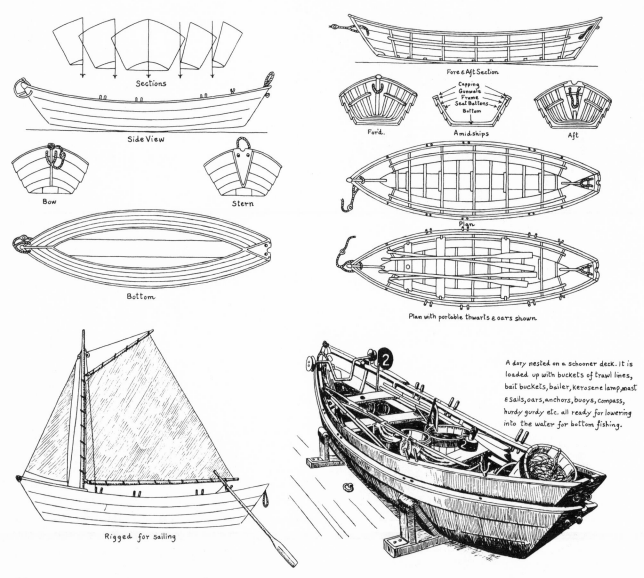

Sections

Side View

Bow

Stern

Bottom

Fore & Aft Section

Capping
Gunwale
Frame
Seat Battens
Bottom

Ford.

Amidships

Aft

Plan

Plan with portable thwarts & oars shown

Rigged for sailing

A dory nested on a schooner deck. It is
loaded up with buckets of trawl lines,
bait buckets, bailer, kerosene lamp, mast
& sails, oars, anchors, buoys, compass,
hurdy gurdy etc. all ready for lowering
into the water for bottom fishing.

The Nova Scotia fishing schooner *Bluenose* became a legend throughout the world in the 1920s as the fastest fishing schooner ever built. Under Captain Angus Walters of Lunenburg, Bluenose consistently won against Gloucester entries in the international fishermen's races of the period. Designed by William Roue of Halifax and built in 1921 by Smith and Rhuland in Lunenburg, the 143-foot vessel was a stirring symbol of the Canadian deep sea heritage.

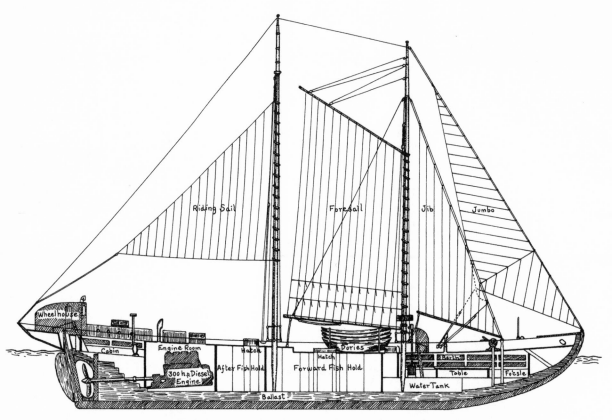

LUNENBURG TYPE DORY-FISHING POWER SCHOONER 1934-1963

These vessels fished "deep sea" summer and winter, using dories with long-line trawls. Many were 145 feet long with a $27\frac{1}{2}$ foot beam and speed of 10 to 12 knots. The crew of 24 to 28 men engaged in fresh fishing in winter and salt fishing in summer. These schooners often remained "hove to" under riding sail or moved about under sail as required when fishing and used the engine for passage.

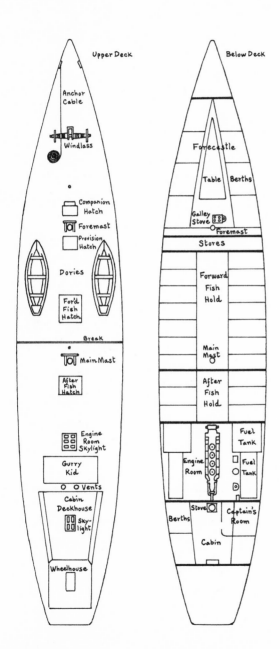

Upper Deck

Anchor Cable

Windlass

Companion Hatch

Foremast

Provision Hatch

Dories

For'd Fish Hatch

Break

Main Mast

After Fish Hatch

Engine Room Skylight

Gurry Kid

Vents

Cabin Deckhouse

Skylight

Wheelhouse

Below Deck

Forecastle

Table   Berths

Galley Stove

Foremast

Stores

Forward Fish Hold

Main Mast

After Fish Hold

Engine Room

Fuel Tank

Fuel Tank

Berths   Stove   Captain's Room

Cabin

Large motor-driven schooners began to replace the sailing vessels on the banks in the 1930s, but they were still dory-fishing schooners perpetuating the schooner tradition.

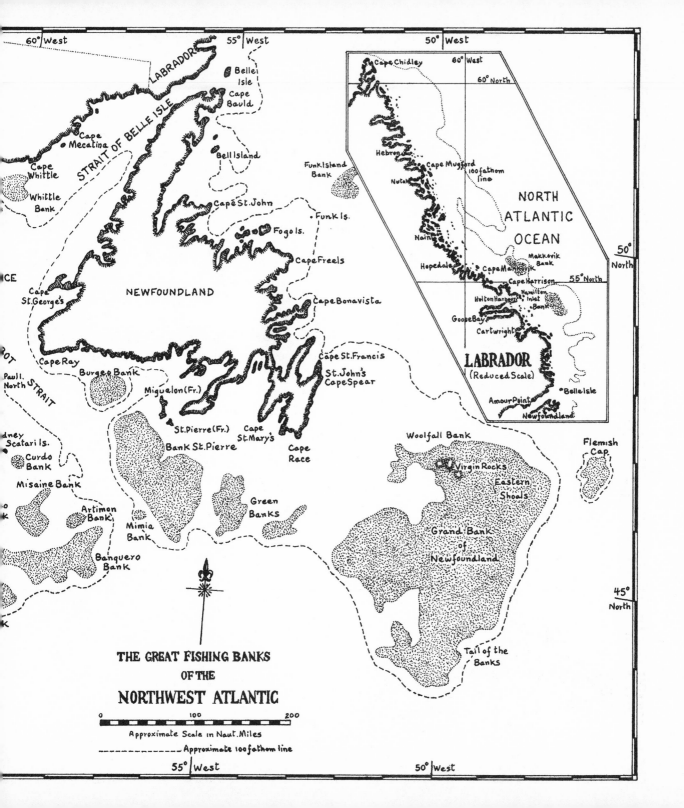

THE GREAT FISHING BANKS
OF THE
NORTHWEST ATLANTIC

The Cape Islanders

The nimble little vessel which is the workhorse of Nova Scotia's large inshore fleets today is the famed Cape Island boat. With distinctive high bows and a long, broad, open workspace, low to the sea, Cape Islanders of various sizes are found everywhere on the Atlantic coast of the province. When fishermen began adopting the gas engine shortly after the turn of the century, they found the deep hulls of inshore sailing craft inefficient for motor propulsion. The Cape Island boat developed in Cape Sable Island eliminated the problem by cutting away the deep hull, making the bottom shallow and nearly flat towards the stern. The style caught on and today there are more Cape Island-type boats built throughout the province than any other kind. On the long Atlantic swells the Cape Islander is sea-kindly, fast and economical. In size, the Cape Island hull ranges from open, powered skiffs to diesel-driven vessels of 40 and 50 feet, with forecastles, cuddys and characteristic wheelhouses bearing modern navigation equipment. Most versatile in the fleet, the Cape Island boat is used in inshore lobstering, longlining, gill-netting, seining, handlining and dragging, as well as raking crops of Irish moss and other seaweeds. For the sea conditions of the Gulf of St. Lawrence, the somewhat different Northumberland Strait boat is popular.

Workhorse of the Nova Scotia inshore fleet is the versatile Cape Island fishing boat.

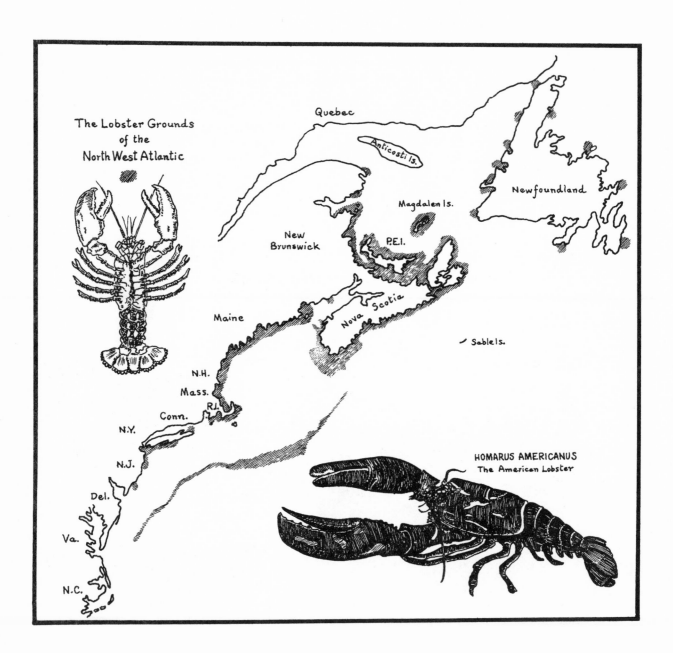

The Lobster Grounds
of the
North West Atlantic

Quebec

Anticosti Is.

Newfoundland

Magdalen Is.

New
Brunswick

P.E.I.

Maine

Nova Scotia

Sable Is.

N.H.

Mass.

R.I.

Conn.

N.Y.

N.J.

Del.

Va.

N.C.

HOMARUS AMERICANUS
The American Lobster

NORTHUMBERLAND STRAIT STYLE FISHERMAN

This typical example, laid up at Cariboo, is 38 feet long, 11 feet beam and 8 feet wide at the stern.

Construction:

These vessels are not caulked. The hulls are constructed from narrow planks, 2 inches wide & 1 inch thick, edge-nailed with galvanized iron nails.

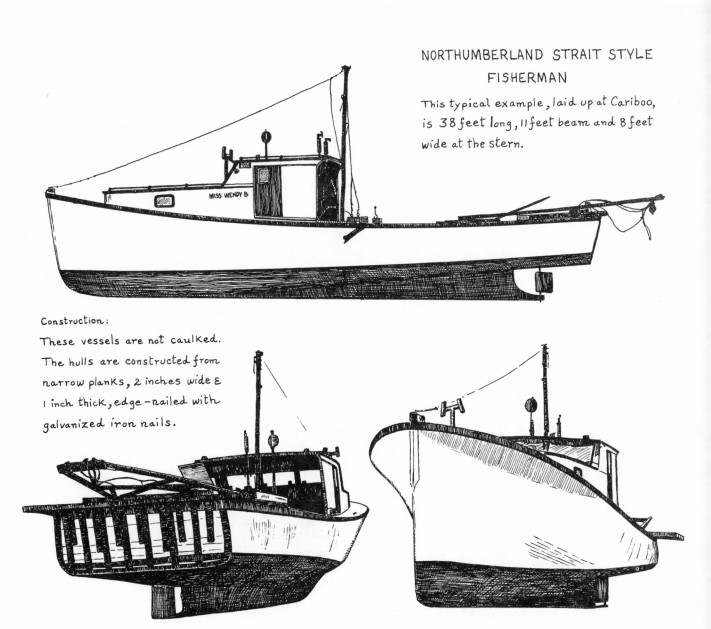

The Nova Scotia Lobster Trap

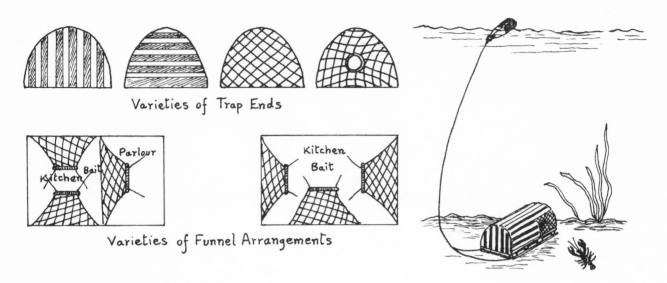

Varieties of Trap Ends

Varieties of Funnel Arrangements

Parlour

Kitchen Bait

Kitchen Bait

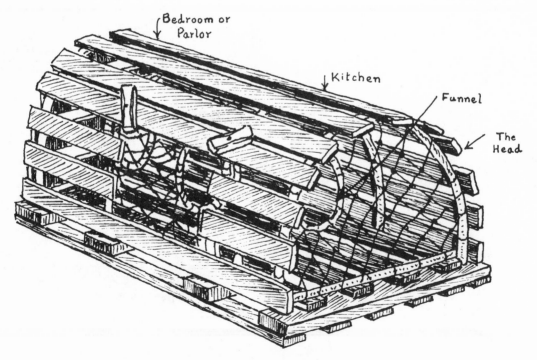

Bedroom or Parlor

Kitchen

Funnel

The Head

St. Margaret's Bay Seines

These attractive lap-work (clinker) boats, built locally, are 28 feet long with an 8 foot beam and are capable of carrying up to 9,000 pounds of fish. They are used to tend the fish traps around the Bay & are considered ideal for handling nets and gear in the relatively sheltered waters of St. Margarets.

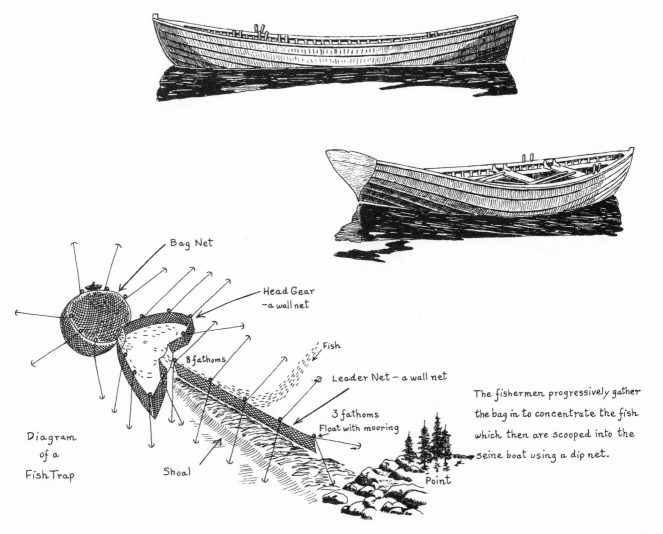

Bag Net

Head Gear — a wall net

Fish

8 fathoms

Leader Net - a wall net

3 fathoms
Float with mooring

Diagram
of a
Fish Trap

Shoal

Point

The fishermen progressively gather the bag in to concentrate the fish which then are scooped into the seine boat using a dip net.

55

Detail of a Fish Net

The Knot used in net-making is the Lock-Knot Sheet Bend. Nets can be made by hand or mended using a plastic or wooden braiding needle or "fiddle" as shown above. Nets either entrap the fish, as in the "cod end" of a trawl, or entangle fish which attempt to swim through the mesh. In the latter case, which is the Gill Net, the mesh is large enough to pass the fish's head and gills but too small for the rest of its body. When the fish tries to back out, its gill covers catch in the mesh. The fish are removed by shaking the net.

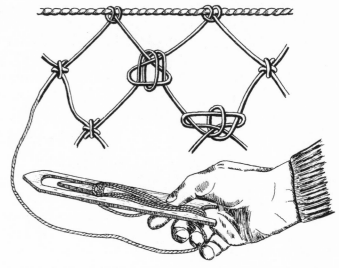

A Fishing Weir in the Bay of Fundy

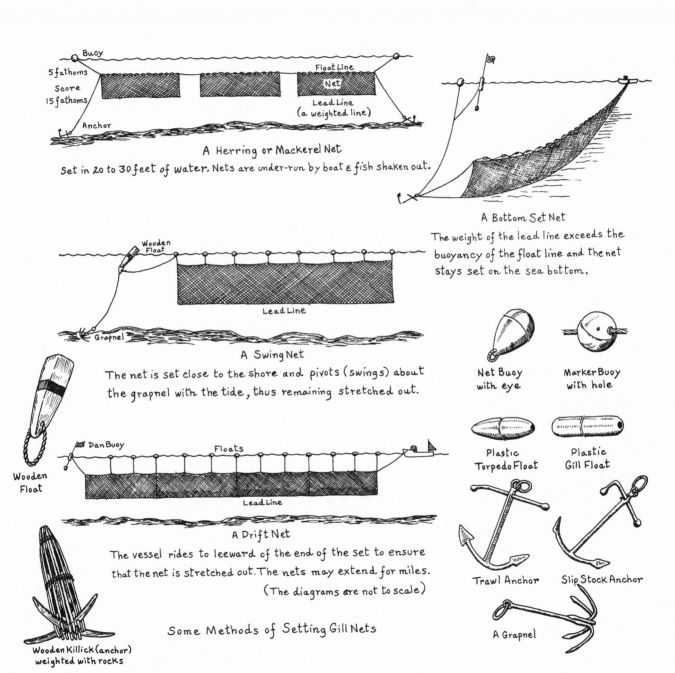

A Herring or Mackerel Net

Buoy

5 fathoms

Score

15 fathoms

Anchor

Float Line

Net

Lead Line
(a weighted line)

Set in 20 to 30 feet of water. Nets are under-run by boat & fish shaken out.

A Bottom Set Net

The weight of the lead line exceeds the buoyancy of the float line and the net stays set on the sea bottom.

Wooden Float

Lead Line

Grapnel

A Swing Net

The net is set close to the shore and pivots (swings) about the grapnel with the tide, thus remaining stretched out.

Net Buoy
with eye

Marker Buoy
with hole

Wooden Float

Dan Buoy

Floats

Lead Line

Plastic
Torpedo Float

Plastic
Gill Float

A Drift Net

The vessel rides to leeward of the end of the set to ensure that the net is stretched out. The nets may extend for miles.

(The diagrams are not to scale)

Trawl Anchor

Slip Stock Anchor

Some Methods of Setting Gill Nets

A Grapnel

Wooden Killick (anchor)
weighted with rocks

Longliners, Seiners and Draggers

Though longlining for groundfish off Nova Scotia is carried out from multi-purpose Cape Islanders and other craft, the larger vessels specializing in longlining come in either of two easily recognized shapes: the traditional double-ender of schooner-like hull with working space forward of the wheelhouse; and the Nova Scotia longliner developed from the Cape Island boat but heavier, and with working space aft. Growing fresh fish markets and the need of inshore fishermen for larger vessels of greater range to extend their fishing season produced more than 100 longliners of 50 to 60 feet in Nova Scotia during the 1950s and longliner construction has continued.

About the same time Nova Scotia's fleet of wooden-hulled draggers of 50 to 70 feet also built up rapidly, and increased in size to 100 feet and over. Many of the smaller draggers were rigged to pull otter-trawl gear over the stern, while those in the 100-foot class were modelled after side trawlers of the period, and capable of otter-trawling or scallop dragging. Vessels of this type form the basis of Nova Scotia's present deep sea scallop fleets. Voyaging to Georges Bank for up to two weeks, the scallop dragger crews of 16 or 17 men average about 30,000 pounds of scallop meats a trip. Seining in Nova Scotia includes Danish as well as pair seining for groundfish, and purse-seining for herring. Large skipper-owned herring seining vessels operate as a mobile fleet in the region.

Some specialized inshore fisheries of Nova Scotia are not based predominantly on vessel usage. These include the stationary weir and trap fisheries for herring and mackerel, which occur in coastal waters from the upper limits of the Bay of Fundy to the northern tip of Cape Breton Island, and the collection of seaweeds and mollusks such as clams, mussels, and the cultivated oysters of the Bras d'Or Lake system and other areas of the province.

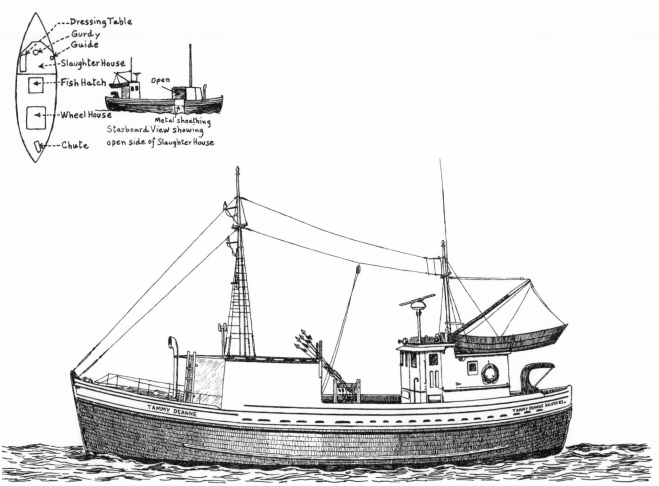

Labels in diagram:
- Dressing Table
- Gurdy
- Guide
- Slaughter House
- Fish Hatch
- Wheel House
- Chute
- Open
- Metal sheathing

Starboard View showing
open side of Slaughter House

TAMMY DEANNE

TAMMY DEANNE HALIFAX N.S.

A 60 foot Double-Ender Longliner

The longline is set through the chute over the stern. A tub filled with coiled
line with baited hooks is placed under the chute and set. The line from the next
tub is knotted to the first line and set in turn; then the third tub and so on until
the set is complete. The line is hauled inboard by a "gurdy" (a vertical winch)
through roller guides on the stb'd. rail amidships into the "slaughter-house"
where the fish are sorted and dressed and the hooks rebaited and the line coiled.

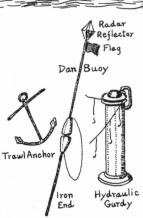

- Radar
- Reflector
- Flag
- Dan Buoy
- Trawl Anchor
- Iron End
- Hydraulic Gurdy

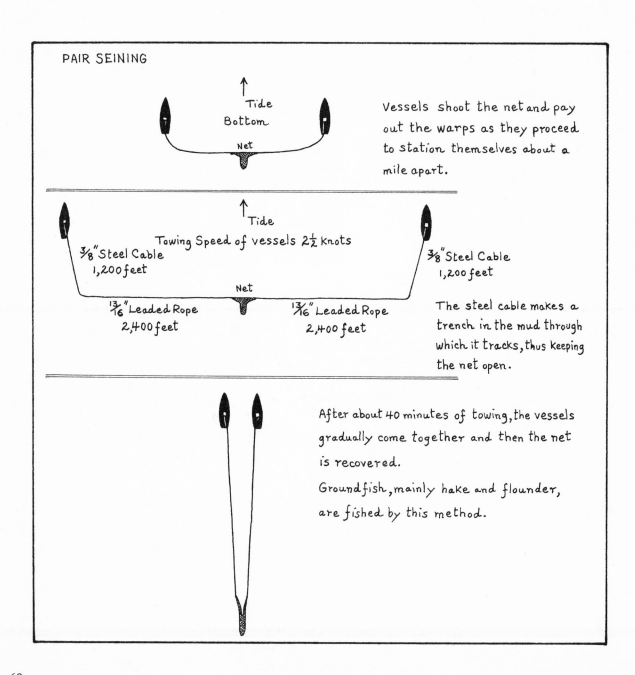

PAIR SEINING

Tide
Bottom

Net

Vessels shoot the net and pay out the warps as they proceed to station themselves about a mile apart.

Tide

Towing Speed of vessels 2½ Knots

$\frac{3}{8}$" Steel Cable
1,200 feet

$\frac{3}{8}$" Steel Cable
1,200 feet

Net

$\frac{13}{16}$" Leaded Rope
2,400 feet

$\frac{13}{16}$" Leaded Rope
2,400 feet

The steel cable makes a trench in the mud through which it tracks, thus keeping the net open.

After about 40 minutes of towing, the vessels gradually come together and then the net is recovered.

Groundfish, mainly hake and flounder, are fished by this method.

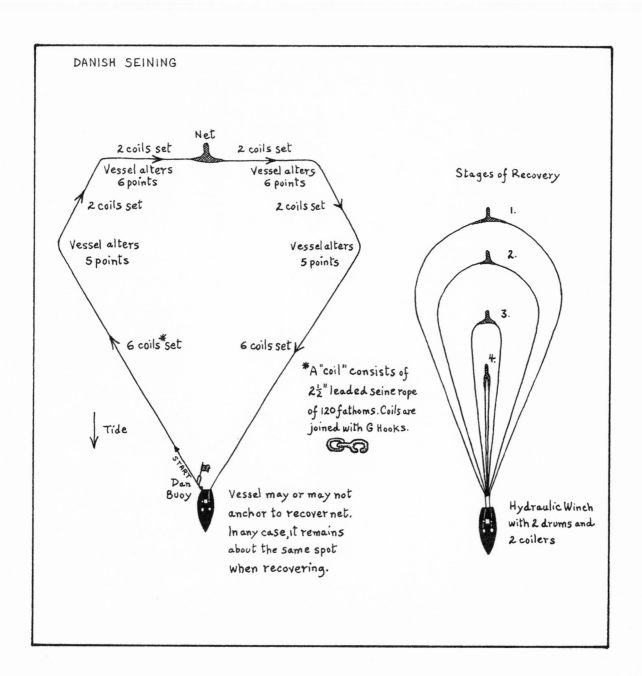

DANISH SEINING

Net

2 coils set →   2 coils set

Vessel alters   Vessel alters
6 points   6 points

↑ 2 coils set   2 coils set ↓

Vessel alters   Vessel alters
5 points   5 points

↑ 6 coils *set   6 coils set ↓

↓ Tide

START
Dan
Buoy

Vessel may or may not
anchor to recover net.
In any case, it remains
about the same spot
when recovering.

*A "coil" consists of
2½" leaded seine rope
of 120 fathoms. Coils are
joined with G Hooks.

Stages of Recovery

1.

2.

3.

4.

Hydraulic Winch
with 2 drums and
2 coilers

61

A Nova Scotian Herring Seiner

A pump on the port side amidships is put into the sea to suck the fish out of the purse seine net. Fish and water are separated inboard, the water goes over the side and the fish chute down the hold. The net is hauled aboard on the starboard side by the power block at the end of the boom (which would be raised). The smaller boom is used for brailing fish from the net when so required. The power skiff is carried on top of the nets bow first on the stern and slid over the transom to set the purse seine net and push the seiner into position. A 60 foot double-ended Herring Carrier shown lying off, works with the Seiner.

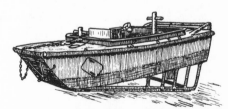

Power Skiff

62

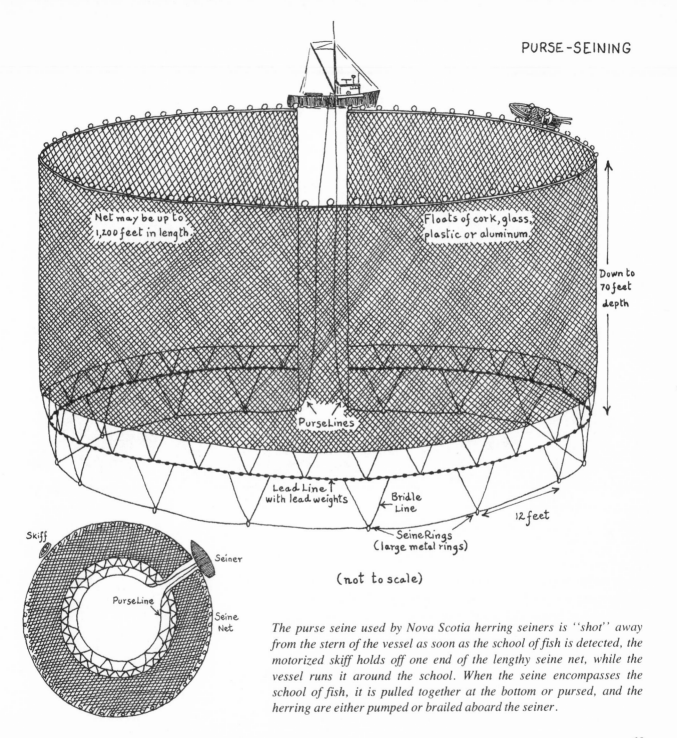

Net may be up to 1,200 feet in length.

Floats of cork, glass, plastic or aluminum.

Down to 70 feet depth

PurseLines

Lead Line with lead weights

Bridle Line

12 feet

Seine Rings (large metal rings)

(not to scale)

Skiff

Seiner

PurseLine

Seine Net

The purse seine used by Nova Scotia herring seiners is ''shot'' away from the stern of the vessel as soon as the school of fish is detected, the motorized skiff holds off one end of the lengthy seine net, while the vessel runs it around the school. When the seine encompasses the school of fish, it is pulled together at the bottom or pursed, and the herring are either pumped or brailed aboard the seiner.

63

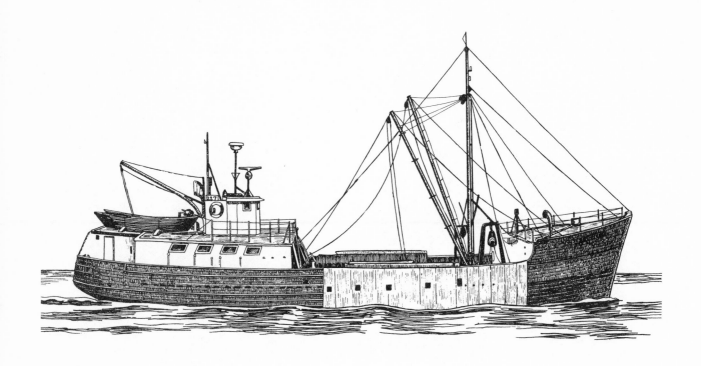

An Offshore Scallop Dragger

The scallop rakes are dragged from the blocks on the gallows, one port & one stb'd. The two booms are used when the rakes are recovered to lift them up so that the contents may be spilled on the deck.

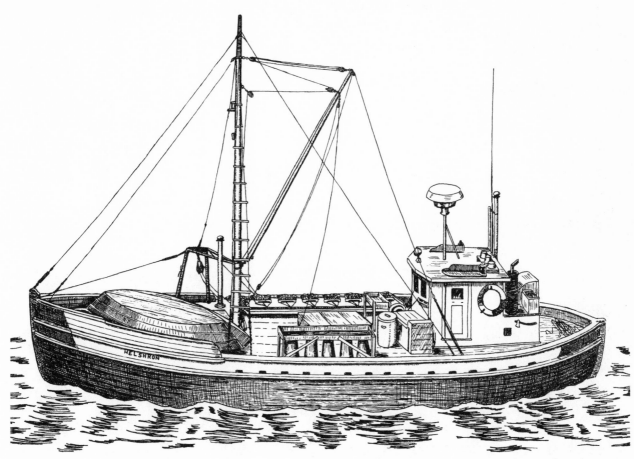

A 50 foot Digby Inshore Scallop Dragger

Scallops are dragged from the sea bottom by 6 or 7 steel mesh bags on a bar towed from a gallows on the starboard side (protected by 3 inch hardwood sheathing). The boom is used for lifting the bags for emptying on to the wooden platform on deck. When the scallops are shucked the wooden platform is tipped up to dump the shells and other debris overboard.

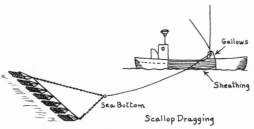

Gallows

Sheathing

Sea Bottom

Scallop Dragging

Scallop bags about to be emptied

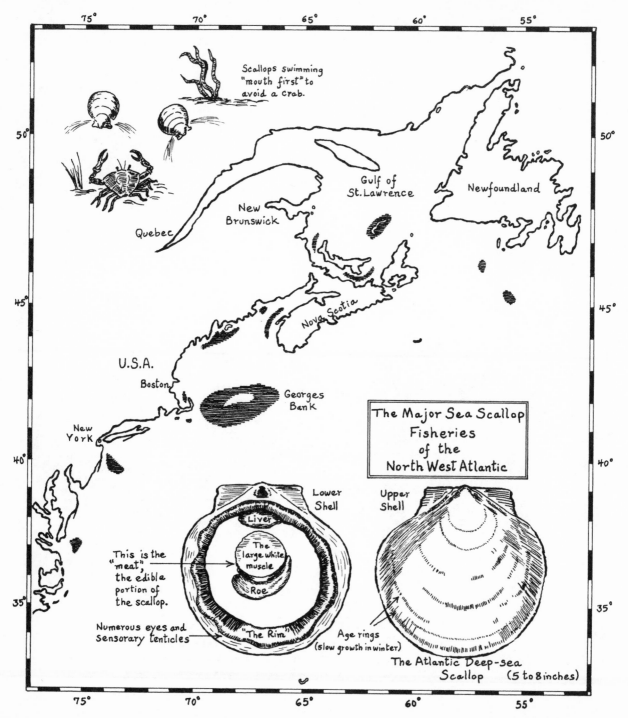

Scallops swimming "mouth first" to avoid a crab.

Gulf of St. Lawrence

Newfoundland

Quebec

New Brunswick

Nova Scotia

U.S.A.

Boston

Georges Bank

New York

The Major Sea Scallop Fisheries of the North West Atlantic

Lower Shell

Liver

The large white muscle

Roe

This is the "meat", the edible portion of the scallop.

Numerous eyes and sensory tenticles

"The Rim"

Upper Shell

Age rings (slow growth in winter)

The Atlantic Deep-sea Scallop   (5 to 8 inches)

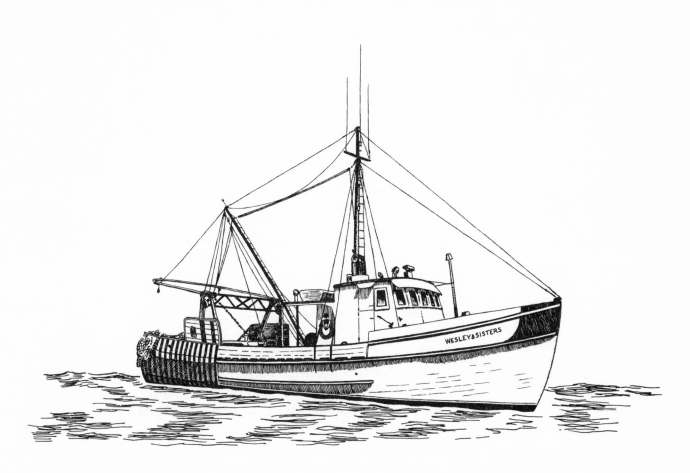

A 60-foot stern dragger used inshore and on the nearer banks for groundfishing with otter-trawl gear. Vessels of this type are also rigged for scallop dragging and longlining.

The Deep Sea Trawlers

Modern stern trawlers are the most efficient deep sea fish catchers, and are the strength of Nova Scotia's present offshore fishing fleets. With crews of 14 men, these steel fishing vessels make trips of 12 to 14 days to the banks and are capable of returning to the processing plants with catches of more than 400,000 pounds of iced groundfish. Most of our present fleet of stern trawlers was built in Nova Scotia in the 1960s and 1970s, beginning soon after this type of vessel was introduced in Europe. The stern trawlers differed radically from the traditional side trawlers which are still in use. The heavy groundfish trawls towed along the bottom from one side of the old trawlers, is towed from the stern of the stern trawlers, providing more efficient deck and handling arrangements and the capability of fishing in heavier weather. Though these stern trawlers in the 150-foot class are small compared to the present European vessels fishing the banks, the Nova Scotia vessels were designed to serve shore-based processing plants and were not required to make ocean crossings. Nova Scotia fishing corporations today are planning a new generation of deep sea fishing trawlers which will include a freezer trawler possibly in the 3,000-ton range, similar to the Europeans vessels. The proposed new freezer trawlers will extend Nova Scotia's offshore capability to fish northern cod as well as species not previously fished commercially by Canadians, including argentine, grenadier, silver hake, capelin and squid, all of which require freezing at sea. Meanwhile, co-operative fishing arrangements with some of the European nations are helping teach our trawlermen the technology of freezer vessel operation. At the same time efforts are underway to develop Canadian export markets for these fish products.

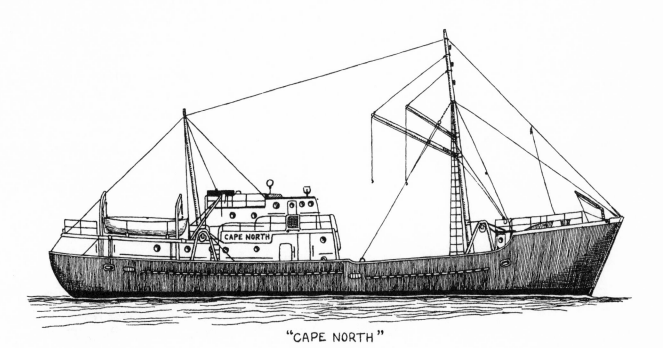

"CAPE NORTH"

The side-trawler Cape North was one of the first Nova Scotia-built wooden trawlers of the port-war period. Now in the Lunenburg Fisheries Museum.

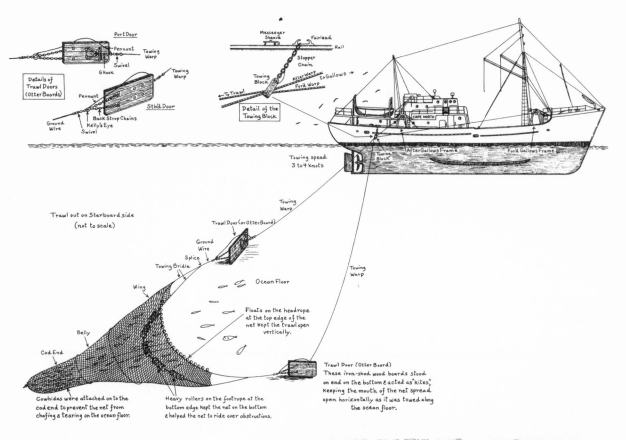

Details of Trawl Doors (Otter Boards)

Port Door
Pennant
Towing Warp
Swivel
G Hook

Stb'd Door
Pennant
Back Strop Chains
Kelly's Eye
Swivel
Ground Wire
Towing Warp

Messenger Sheave
Fairlead
Rail
Stopper Chain
Towing Block
After Warp
To Gallows
Ford Warp
To Trawl

Detail of the Towing Block.

CAPE NORTH

Towing Block
After Gallows Frame
Ford Gallows Frame

Towing speed 3 to 4 knots

Towing Block

Trawl out on Starboard side (not to scale)

Towing Warp

Trawl Door (or Otter Board)
Ground Wire
Splice
Towing Bridle
Wing
Ocean Floor
Belly
Cod End

Floats on the headrope at the top edge of the net kept the trawl open vertically.

Towing Warp

Trawl Door (Otter Board)
These iron-shod wood boards stood on end on the bottom & acted as "kites", keeping the mouth of the net spread open horizontally as it was towed along the ocean floor.

Cowhides were attached on to the cod end to prevent the net from chafing & tearing on the ocean floor.

Heavy rollers on the footrope at the bottom edge kept the net on the bottom & helped the net to ride over obstructions.

The wheelhouse of the stern trawler Cape Argos illustrating electronic navigation and fish-finding gear. This Nova Scotia vessel was the first North American mid-water trawler.

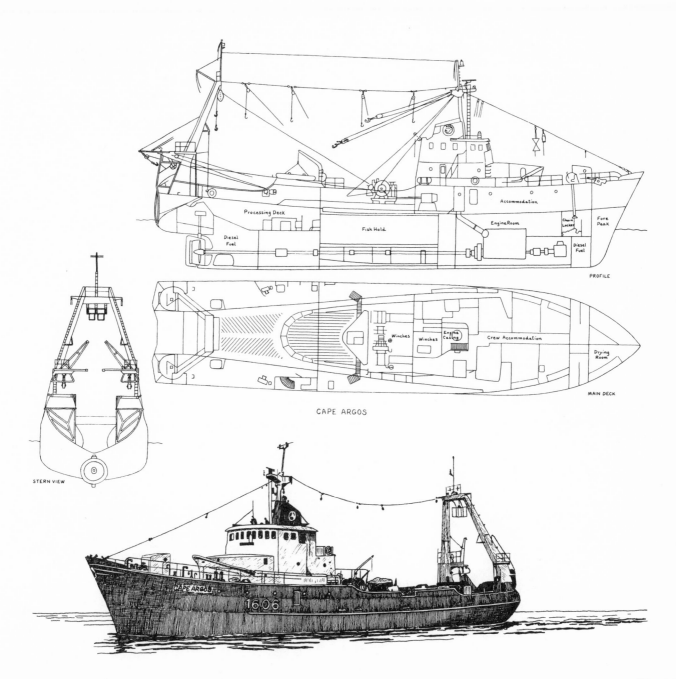

Processing Deck

Accommodation

Diesel
Fuel

Fish Hold

Engine Room

Chain
Locker

Fore
Peak

Diesel
Fuel

PROFILE

Winches

Winches

Engine
Casing

Crew Accommodation

Drying
Room

MAIN DECK

STERN VIEW

CAPE ARGOS

CAPE ARGOS

1606

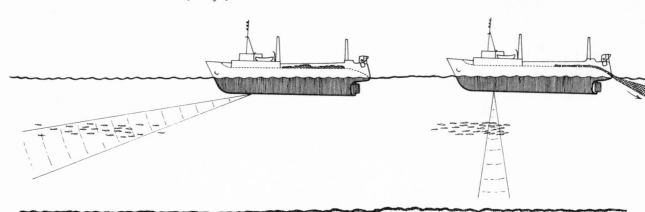

School of fish detected by Sonar.
The Sonar has a range of up to 2 miles and
can search step by step either 360° or in a
smaller sector as desired.

Trawler alters course to intercept the school.
Sonar is a beam of pulses of sound, which on
striking an object such as a school of fish,
returns an echo to be detected by the ship.

Trawler shoots her trawl. Sonar beam tilts down
as required to continue tracking the fish.
When the trawler passes over the school, the
depth of the fish is confirmed by echo sounder.

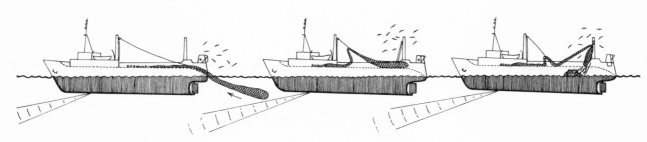

Hauling in the Trawl   The Cod End on Deck   Emptying the Trawl
                                                                       through the opened hatch
                                                                       into fish pounds on the deck
                                                                       below

The Pelagic Trawl

Pelagic refers to those varieties of fish which live in
midwater and are not catchable with ground trawls.
The Pelagic Trawl is much larger than a Bottom Trawl.
It is made up of a top half and a bottom half and two
side panels i.e. four large tapering pieces with long wings.
A standard design is not fixed as yet.

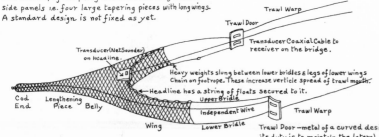

Trawl Warp

Trawl Door

Transducer Coaxial Cable to
receiver on the bridge.

Transducer (Net Sounder)
on Headline.

Heavy weights slung between lower bridles & legs of lower wings
Chain on footrope. These increase verticle spread of trawl mouth.

Headline has a string of floats secured to it.

Upper Bridle

Cod   Lengthening   Belly
End   Piece

Wing   Independent Wire   Trawl Warp

Lower Bridle

Trawl Door — metal of a curved design,
its duty is to maintain the lateral
spread of the mouth of the net.

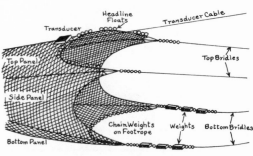

Detail of Mouth of Pelagic Trawl

Headline Floats
Transducer
Transducer Cable
Top Panel
Top Bridles
Side Panel
Chain Weights on Footrope
Weights
Bottom Bridles
Bottom Panel

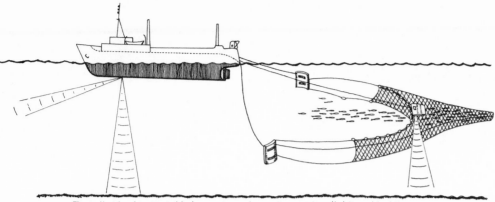

The depth of trawl is adjusted by increasing or decreasing speed so that the net is at the same depth as the school of fish. This is "aimed trawling." A net sounder on the head rope monitors the depth of the net.

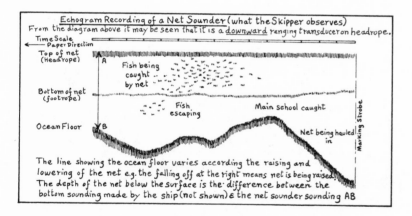

Echogram Recording of a Net Sounder (what the Skipper observes)

From the diagram above it may be seen that it is a downward ranging transducer on headrope.

Time Scale
← Paper Direction

Top of net (Headrope) — A

Fish being caught by net

Bottom of net (footrope)

Fish escaping — Main school caught

Ocean Floor — B

Net being hauled in

Marking Strobe

The line showing the ocean floor varies according the raising and lowering of the net e.g. the falling off at the right means net is being raised. The depth of the net below the surface is the difference between the bottom sounding made by the ship (not shown) & the net sounder sounding AB

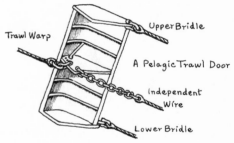

Trawl Warp
Upper Bridle
A Pelagic Trawl Door
Independent Wire
Lower Bridle

The mid-water trawl is used by Nova Scotia trawlermen principally to catch redfish on the slopes of the offshore banks. The trawl is about 500 feet long and held in the mid-water position by the speed of the vessel. A transducer attached by cable to the trawl transmits information on the elevation of the trawl and other data to the bridge.

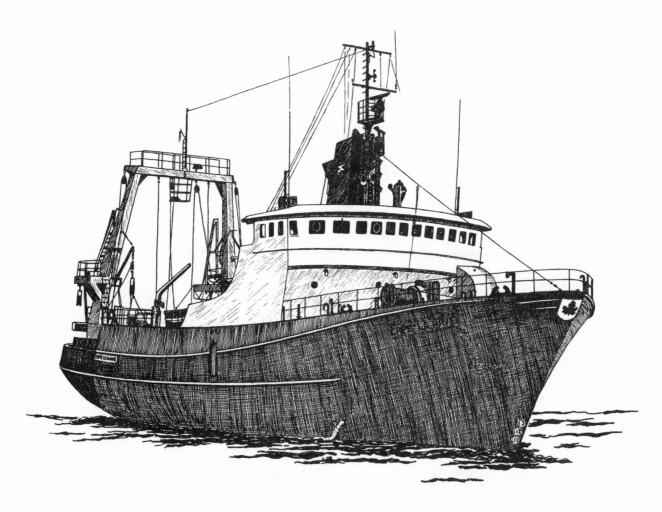

"CAPE LA HAVE"

The modern stern trawler Cape LaHave, built in 1973 and capable of carrying over 400,000 pounds of fish from the offshore banks.

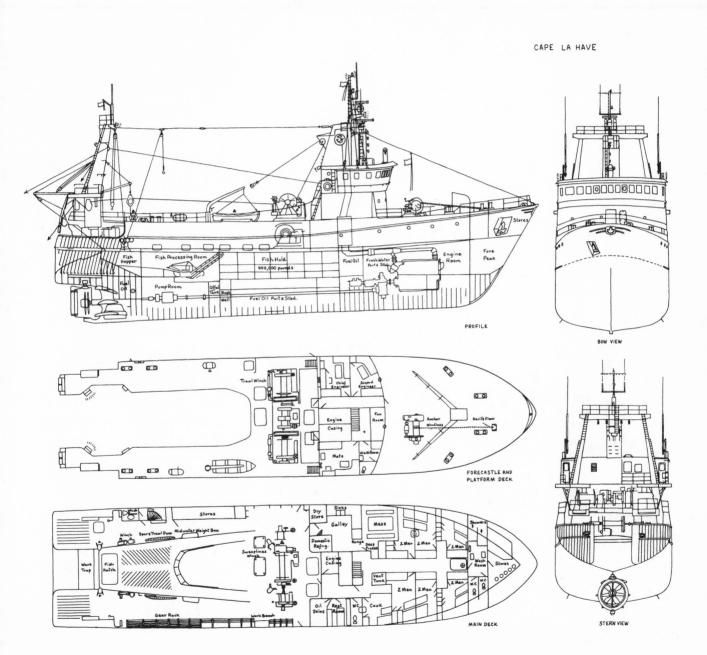

CAPE LA HAVE

PROFILE

Fish Hopper

Fish Processing Room

Fish Hold
400,000 pounds

Fuel Oil

FreshWater Port & Stbd.

Engine Room

Fore Peak

Stores

Fuel Oil

Pump Room

Offal Tank

Slush Well

Fuel Oil Port & Stbd.

BOW VIEW

FORECASTLE AND PLATFORM DECK

Trawl Winch

Chief Engineer

Second Engineer

Engine Casing

Fan Room

Anchor Windlass

Devils Claw

Mate

Washroom

MAIN DECK

Wash

Stores

Dry Store

Sinks

Galley

Mess

Showers

Winch

Spare Trawl Door

Midwater Weight Box

Domestic Refrig.

Range

Deep Freeze

2 Man

2 Man

2 Man

Sweeplines Winch

Wash Room

Stores

Work Trap

Fish Hatch

Engine Casing

Vent Trunk

2 Man

2 Man

2 Man

W.C.

W.C.

Oil Skins

Rest Room

W.C.

Cook

Gear Rack

Work Bench

STERN VIEW

75

Where the Fish Come From

GROUNDFISH

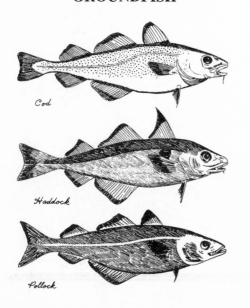

Cod

Haddock

Pollock

The great sea-fishing grounds of the Northwest Atlantic curve down the face of the globe in a watery arc half the length of the continent, from the chill silences of the Labrador Sea to the hook of Cape Cod and beyond. In the calibrations of geological time, these offshore fishing grounds or "banks" are recent phenomena: a creation of the last ice age. The Nova Scotia Banks, the Grand Banks of Newfoundland, the Labrador Banks, and Georges Bank off New England, are actually a series of vast submarine plateaus, rising from the submerged coastal plain which forms our extensive eastern continental shelf.

As glacial ice retreated from the coast of Nova Scotia some 18 thousand years ago, ocean levels rose inundating the ancient coastal plain and leaving the plateaus as a chain of islands until these too were submerged to become the offshore banks. From a hundred thousand square miles of these undersea landscapes, creased with valleys, slopes and canyons, the trawlermen occasionally bring home fossil momentoes of epochs before this country was returned to the ocean. The banks are large: ranging from the 3,000 square miles of Banquereau, one of the Nova Scotia Banks, to Georges' 8,500 square miles, and the great sweep of the Grand Bank which is the biggest. Covering 37 thousand square miles, it is 200 miles wide and 350 miles long, and larger in area than all of Newfoundland.

Corresponding to the offshore banks are those nearer the coasts, which can be worked by fishermen using smaller boats than the offshore draggers and trawlers. And all around the thousands of miles of sea-combed coastline are the traditional inshore grounds. These are the myriad shoal waters and ledges worked daily by the fishermen from hundreds of small coastal villages — when the fish are there and the weather holds up.

Two mammoth rivers of the ocean give life to the offshore banks, as well as the fishing grounds inshore. The warm Gulf Stream, driven by prevailing winds and the earth's rotation, with a thousand times the volume of the greatest rivers of the land, flows north from the Caribbean, near the edge of the continental shelf, to meet the cold Labrador Current streaming down from the Arctic. The warm salt sea from the tropics striking the chill brackish waters of the Labrador Current generates a broad band of boundary waters of intermediate temperature and salinity along the slope of the continental shelf, the outer edge of the offshore banks. The inshore waters of Nova Scotia in summer consist entirely of the upper layer of water from the Scotian Shelf. This layer may be as much as 40 fathoms thick and has temperatures ranging from 5C (41F) to 20C (68F). The same slope water at a somewhat lower temperature also invades the inshore side of the Grand Bank. Meanwhile, the cold Labrador Current floods the Grand Bank at depth, skirts its southern tail and flows westward towards the Nova Scotia Banks. This produces complex currents and layering in which waters at mid-depth are colder than surface and bottom waters. It is this cold mid-layer that conditions Nova Scotia's offshore banks.

When the northern hemisphere of earth begins tilting towards the sun with the new year, the gradual unfolding of spring from south to north brings with it the exotic flowering of the phytoplankton. Over thousands of square miles of ocean, the pale blue carpet of billions upon billions of these mainly miscroscopic sea plants stretches across the banks. Feeding on the nitrates and other minerals welling up with the currents from the depths, the phytoplankton multiply, converting the energy of the sun into plant material, to form the first link in the food chain of the

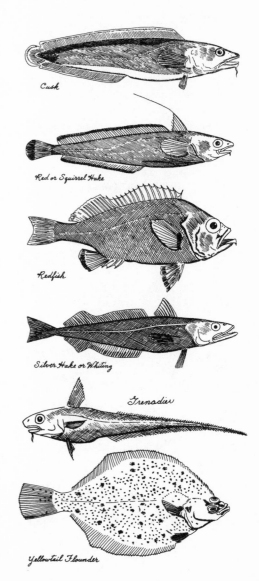

Cusk

Red or Squirrel Hake

Redfish

Silver Hake or Whiting

Grenadier

Yellowtail Flounder

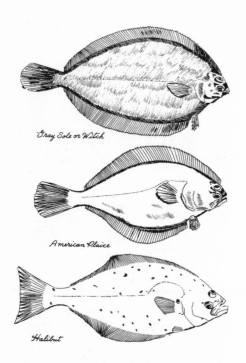

Gray Sole or Witch

American Plaice

Halibut

PELAGIC & ESTUARIAL

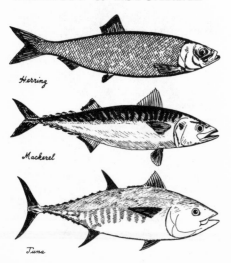

Herring

Mackerel

Tuna

oceans. Feeding on this plant life are the zooplankton, which are the secondary production level on which the larvae and adults of many species feed.

On this coast the cod is king. Some of the other sea creatures may bring more money per pound today, but the sovereignty of the Atlantic cod has remained unshaken since the beginning of the fisheries here in the early 16th century. Indeed the Northwest Atlantic fisheries is still built upon the prolific and voracious Atlantic cod, though many other important species of fish, crustaceans, mollusks and seaweeds are also taken. Among fishermen, traditionally the word fish meant cod. Other species might be called by their proper names, such as haddock, tuna or halibut, but only the cod was fish. This mark of the cod's status in the fishing industry was once written into some of the laws on this coast.

The life of the Atlantic cod begins with spawning in the cold waters at depths of 350 to 600 feet, over widely separated areas of the banks and shelf, and at varying times of year from south to north. While the cod spawns on Georges Bank in November and December, on Sable Island Bank they spawn in March and April, and on Grand Bank from April to June. Though a female may produce three or four million eggs, only one in a million of the young is likely to survive and become a mature fish. The buoyant fertilized eggs, a little over a millimetre in size, rise to the surface, incubate, and hatch out the tiny larval cod.

Less than a quarter-inch long at the beginning, the larval and cod dwells in the plankton pastures of the ocean feeding on those minute plankton animals and the larvae of lobsters, shrimps and barnacles. If it survives the surface predators, the little fish is over an inch long at two months and ready for its dangerous migration to the bottom to join the adult cod and forage for itself.

Many sea fish, such as haddock, cusk, hake and pollock, as well as the halibut and other flat fish, begin life in the same way. The herring spawns inshore, and the Atlantic salmon, shad, gaspereau and smelt spawn up the rivers and creeks away from the sea, while the young of the redfish and porbeagle are born live.

As a demersal or groundfish, the cod dwells and feeds near the bottom, on a highly varied diet including mollusks, crabs, shrimp, small lobsters, herring, capelin, sand lance, squid, and occasionally any seabird it can catch. Indeed, the early fishermen often used the flesh of the flightless and now extinct Great Auk for bait — as well as a change of diet for themselves.

Seasonal migrations of the major cod populations on the Nova Scotia Banks are not so great as in the Gulf of St. Lawrence where the cod in winter move seaward into deeper water, and on the Labrador shelf where they migrate to the more southerly banks. The cod on New England's Nantucket Shoals also migrate south for the winter, as far as North Carolina. However, these movements don't compare with the ocean voyaging of some pelagic or surface-feeding fish, such as the salmon or bluefin tuna.

The average weight of the mature cod taken in the commercial fishery today is about five pounds and the cod seldom exceeds 60 pounds though historical records show 200-pound fish. They grow at different rates in different areas of the banks. One reason the English preferred the Avalon peninsula in the 17th century was its relatively small size of cod which suited their dry salt curing methods.

Of the great range and volume of marine life on our continental shelf, both on the offshore fishing banks and inshore, the commercial fishermen of Nova Scotia today

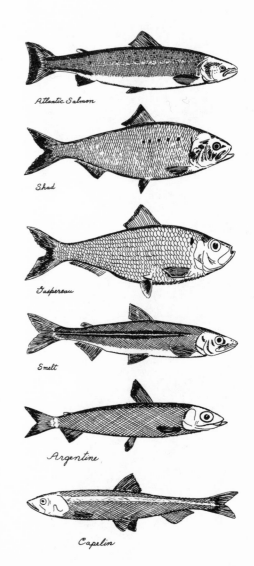

Atlantic Salmon

Shad

Gaspereau

Smelt

Argentine

Capelin

CRUSTACEANS

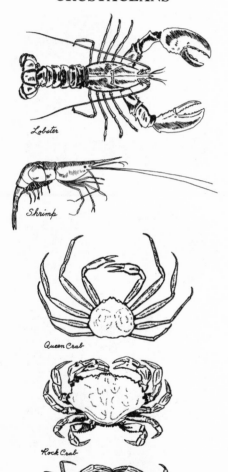

Lobster

Shrimp

Queen Crab

Rock Crab

Deep Sea Red Crab

take less than 20 different kinds of fish. Their catch of food-fish is determined naturally by the availability of stocks, but also by established consumer preferences, commercial demand and day-to-day prices. Similar conditions apply to the fishing fleets of the other Canadian Atlantic provinces, New Brunswick, Prince Edward Island and Newfoundland; as well as Quebec and New England.

In both volume and dollar value to the fisherman, codfish is usually the biggest item in Nova Scotia's annual groundfish catch. Once called "the beef of the sea", cod is long established as an important staple commodity in international markets, and tends to rule the groundfish economy.

The most recent figures of Environment Canada show that Nova Scotia fishermen in 1976 landed 50,952 metric tons, or more than 103 million pounds of codfish, worth nearly $12.5 million to them. Actual market value of that cod was about $25 million. Of the other groundfish: haddock, pollock, hake, cusk and redfish, the haddock sold for the highest price so that just over 19 thousand metric tons brought well over $8 million, while the redfish catch of nearly 35 thousand metric tons, brought over $4.4 million. The halibut catch of 928 metric tons gave fishermen nearly $1.7 million, and the catch of other flatfish — plaice, grey sole and yellowtail flounders — totalled 17,899 metric tons bringing over $3.7 million. Among the pelagic and estuarial fish, including herring, mackerel, smelt, shad, gaspereau, salmon and tuna, Nova Scotia fishermen in 1976 caught more herring than anything else, landing 96,290 metric tons worth over $6.4 million. The total volume of all the fin-fish — groundfish as well as pelagic and estuarial — was 270,041 metric tons with a landed value to the fishermen of more than $44.8 million.

Equally valuable to Nova Scotia fishermen as the finfish, however, are the large crustacean and mollusk fisheries. Scallop vessels brought home 89,419 metric tons of scallops in 1976, worth more than $36.9 million. The lobster catch totalled 5,690 metric tons valued at about $21,000,000. Shrimps, crabs, clams and oysters make up the balance of these fisheries. The total volume for 1976 was 97,842 metric tons or 215,704,430 pounds, valued at $59.8 million. In addition, Nova Scotia's seaweeds industry produced 10,726 metric tons of Irish moss worth nearly $1 million.

This brings the total volume of Nova Scotia sea fisheries in 1976 to 367,883 metric tons or 813,041,219 pounds (not including seaweeds) worth $104,692,000 to the fishermen of Nova Scotia, and about twice that figure in market value.

With a long tradition of efficient and aggressive fishing, the Nova Scotians are the most successful fishermen living along this coast. Of the five Canadian provinces and five New England states fishing in the Northwest Atlantic grounds, Nova Scotia stood first in 1976 in both total catch and landed value. Next in place were Newfoundland with over 747 million pounds at $62 million, and Massachusetts (1975 figures) with 269 million pounds worth $78 million.

MOLLUSKS

Bar or Surf Clam

Soft-Shell Clam

Scallop

Quahog

Ocean Quahog

European Flat Oyster

Native Oyster

Whelk

Blue Mussel

Periwinkle

SEAWEED

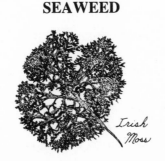

Irish Moss

SQUID

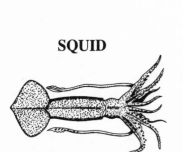

Home from the Tide

Of Nova Scotia's 10,500 fishermen, only 3,000 man the deep sea trawler and dragger fleets, and all the rest are inshore fishermen, full time or part of the time, operating or crewing in anything from trap-tending seine boats to the multi-purpose Cape Islanders, and the smaller longliners, seiners and draggers which fish the inner banks and shoal waters. For the inshore waters their boats, with intermediate technology, are more efficient than the larger vessels. And in terms of costs per pound of fish landed, the Nova Scotians, inshore and offshore, are among the world's most efficient fishermen.

Though the offshore and inshore fisheries are technically different, Nova Scotia fishermen are frequently involved in both. A Westport lobster fisherman, for example, finishes the winter lobster season in his Cape Island boat off Digby Neck, and spends the rest of the year crewing in a large Saulnierville herring seiner.

In the offshore fleets, all Nova Scotia captains and deck officers rise through the ranks from deckhands, and are trained in modern navigation and ship operation at the Nova Scotia Fisheries Training Centre in Pictou. But for success on the banks knowledge of fish and fish-catching is important and often more difficult than running a vessel. One Halifax fishing executive claims that a good trawler skipper really has to think like a fish.

Pay for the most successful skippers in the offshore fleets is good: from $30,000 to $50,000 for the highliners, or those catching the most fish. Pay for their officers and crew can run from $12,000 to $32,000. Some deckhands in the offshore scallop fleet in 1976 made as high as $28,000. Inshore, the fisherman's income depends largely on the size of his enterprise. A fisherman owning and operating a $300,000 fish dragger and employing a crew of three or four, is running a business that may pay him the equal of some offshore scalloper or trawler skippers. Some inshore fishermen, lobstering and handlining with small boat and gear, may make less than $10,000 and part time fishermen may make less than that.

Like agriculture, fishing is perceived as a way of life, and comparisons with urban industrial employment are hard to make. Fishing is not only our oldest industry, it is one of the oldest activities of man, surviving from the ancient hunting cultures. Our Micmac Indians fished the bays and estuaries though not the seas.

The fishing communities are predominantly rural in character. Activities onshore are centred around the wharves and the fish plants. The fisherman's "fields" stretch to the horizon of the sea and beyond. Inshore and offshore the work is taxing, requires many skills, long hours, and quick judgement based on lengthy experience. Fishing in many Nova Scotia families goes back for generations. Most fishermen today began as boys working in the inshore boats on school holidays, or signing up for the summer as a learner or hand aboard a trawler. They say the sea gets into their blood. In any case, few fishermen willingly leave the occupation.

In terms of employment, fishing is the largest single industry in Nova Scotia. In all, some 15,000 people work in the fisheries — including about 4,500 plant workers. The value of primary production in the fisheries of Nova Scotia is greater than agriculture and forestry combined. Many of the trawlermen and plant workers belong to industrial unions. Collective bargaining has been discussed among some fishermen, but the principal organization of the independent inshore fishermen is the Nova Scotia Fishermen's Association.

Scots Bay
Ross Creek
Baxter's Harbour
Hall's Harbour
Canada Creek
Harbourville
Morden

Joggins
Apple River
Advocate Hbr.
Spencer's Island
Port Greville
Diligent River
Black Rock
Parrsboro
Five Islands
Economy
Delhaven
Kingsport
Summerville
Gaspereau

Margaretsville
Port George
Port Lorne
Hampton
Young Cove
Parker's Cove
Hillsburn
Delap Cove
Victoria Beach
Port Wade
Karsdale
Granville Ferry

Culloden
Griffin's Brook
Centreville
Sandy Cove
Mink Cove
New Edinburgh
Little River
Whale Cove
Tiddville
East Ferry
Weymouth
Tiverton
Long Island
Freeport
Westport
Church Point
Comeauville
Meteghan — Saulnierville
Bear Cove
St. Alphonse
Cape St. Mary
Salmon River
Port Maitland
Short Beach
Sandford
Chegoggin
Overton
Yarmouth
Yarmouth Bar
Kelly Cove
Rockville
Chebogue
Chebogue Point
Cook Beach
Pinkney Point
Little River Harbour
Ellenwood Island
Deep Cove Island
John's Island
Turpentine Island
Tusket
Hubbard Point
Sluice Point
Surette Island
Upper Wedgeport
Wedgeport
Lower Wedgeport
Argyle & Eel Brook
Lower Argyle
Pubnico
West Pubnico
Middle West Pubnico
Lower West Pubnico
East Pubnico
Middle East Pubnico
Lower East Pubnico
Abbot's Harbour

ANNAPOLIS
Digby
DIGBY
Saulnierville

Woods Harbour
Shag Harbour
Lower Clark's Hbr.
Swim Point
Clark's Harbour
West Head
Newellton
Bear Point
Doctor's Cove
The Hawk
South Side
Stony Island
Clam Point
North East Point
Sherose Island
West Baccaro
Baccaro
Port La Tour
Upper Port La Tour

LUN
QUEENS
Liverpool
YARMOUTH
Yarmouth
SHELBURNE
Shelburne
Mud Island

NorthWest Hbr.
Ingomar
Gunning Cove
Shelburne
Sandy Point
Jordan Bay
Jordan Falls
West Green Hbr.
Lockeport
Pleasant Point
Little Harbour
Jones Harbour
West Port Hebert
East Port Hebert
Central Port Mouton
Port Mouton
Hunts Point
Moose Harbour
Liverpool

This map indicates most of Nova Scotia's hundreds of fishing ports, but not necessarily all. Furthermore, many fishermen live in communities near the coast which are not considered ports.

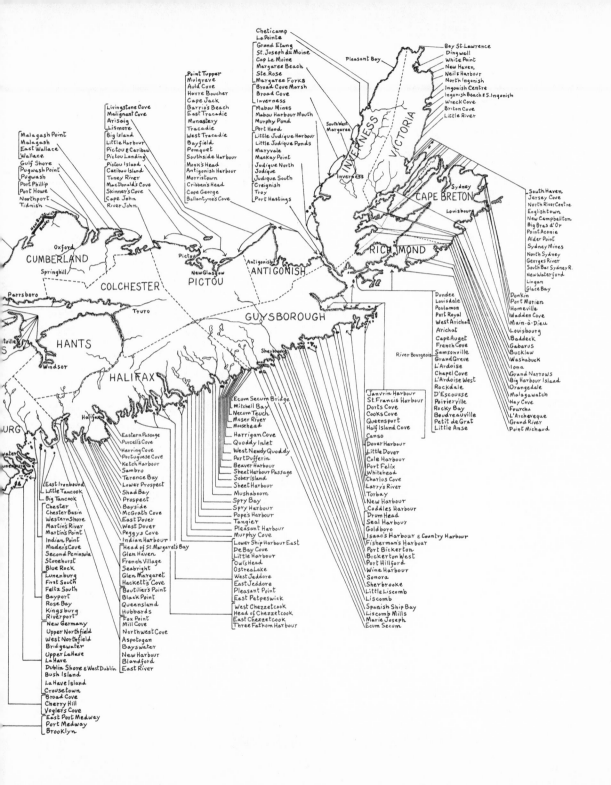

The Business of Fishing

In the hundreds of fishing communities nestled among the innumerable glittering harbours and coves around the coast of Nova Scotia, one of the most important and traditional institutions is the local fish company. Of 186 fish buying and processing firms in Nova Scotia, at least 150 of them are small or medium-sized local enterprises, serving fishermen in their own particular regions. The small independent fish firms, employing local management and labour, are economic mainstays in many of our coastal communities.

The entrepreneurs and managers who run the competitive local fish firms are often tough-minded traders who grew up in the fish business and, from a regional point of view, know it better than anyone else. Their plants, old and new, are part of the unique waterfront architecture of Nova Scotia. From Dingwall to Digby Neck the prim and practical frame buildings crowd village wharves and seafronts with the intricate business of the sea fisheries, which is coupled with international trade and transport.

A vital component of the overall processing and marketing operations of Nova Scotia fisheries, the small local firms often work side-by-side with the large, integrated seafood industries in the province that catch and process most of the groundfish. While the large firms run their own fleets of offshore groundfish trawlers and scallop draggers, the small firms seldom own vessels, but depend instead on the smaller fisherman-owned boats, many of which are in the inshore fleet — and not more than 65 feet in length.

Though the large seafood industries also serve the inshore fisherman, buying his fish and selling him fishing supplies, directly or through regional branch plants, the bulk of their groundfish supplies comes from their own offshore fleets, and they are not dependent upon the inshore fishermen as the smaller local firms are. As fisheries industries, the different-sized firms are more complementary than antagonistic. The small independents may perform as feeder plants or purchase from the larger firms as needed and, though they may sometimes compete for fish supplies, they seldom compete directly for sales in the same market areas.

Nevertheless, the small and medium sized firms are perceived as being closer to the inshore fishery because of the identification with their local fishing communities, their accessibility, scale, and ultimate dependence upon the inshore fishermen.

With the larger proportion of the fisheries in the counties of southwestern Nova Scotia bordering the Atlantic, most of the small independent firms are located there. On the southwest coast the inshore fishery is the strongest and most diversified in Atlantic Canada. Historically, the small independents evolved from the same sources that built up the inshore fleets in this area at the turn of the century: the proximity and continuing connection with United States markets, the traditional high competence of the local people in both fishing and trading, and the continuing diversity if not abundance of inshore fish stocks.

Elsewhere in the province the small independent fish firms were established for similar reasons, often by dedicated local entrepreneurs who recognized the private business opportunity in serving the regional fishery and assisting in its development. In an enterprise like the fisheries, however, with a highly perishable product, open to fluctuations in supply and subject to shifting markets and prices, historically failures, mergers and take-overs have not been uncommon.

Yet, a great many survive, and their service to the

fisheries and the fishing communities of Nova Scotia appears to be indispensable. Their role in the overall organization of the fishery industry embraces fish buying, gear supply, a wide range of fish processing, warehousing, packaging, marketing, transportation and domestic and export sales.

That little fish plant down on the wharf may be processing one or two million pounds of groundfish a year, as fresh fillets and frozen blocks; or salt fish, dried in temperature-controlled chambers to the moisture preferences of various markets. It may also be filleting herring, smoking kippers and bloaters, and handling lobsters in season or from the firm's own lobster pound. The diversity reflects market and supply opportunities and is also a hedge against individual species fluctuations.

The value added locally in the processing of fin fish more than doubles their price between the wharf and the marketplace. Most of the selling is simply done by long distance telephone between the manager and the firm's agent or broker in the marketing centres of Boston, New York, Montreal or Toronto. The conversations are casual, as if between old friends. Basically, the prices are established by the open market, with local variations. Orders are confirmed by mail. In the fresh fish trade, cargoes of fillets may be sold before the draggers and longliners reach port. From radio information the manager knows their catch, estimated time of arrival, and the processing, packing and transit time required to deliver the fish in, say, Boston. With good highway access to every coastal community in Nova Scotia, nearly all fish today is transported in large refrigerated tractor-trailers carrying up to 20 thousand pounds a trip.

Like the inshore fleets they primarily serve, the small

production units of the independent local firms are efficient when the fish are in good supply and markets are reasonable. Operating with low overheads, they are sensitive and responsive to local conditions and opportunities. But their resilience is limited. Because of their size they are less able than the larger industries to cope with economic and environmental disasters, such as the depletion of fish stocks in the 1970s on the Scotian shelf.

Ironically, it was the failure of the small private firms, in the depression years of the 1920s and 1930s, to serve adequately the fishermen of eastern Nova Scotia that helped launch the Maritime Co-operative Movement. Led by parish priests and teachers, the fishermen formed producer co-operatives which were forerunners of the United Maritime Fishermen. With branches and affiliated fishermen's co-operatives throughout Nova Scotia and the

Fish stages for drying cod at Lunenburg in the 1930s have been replaced long since by modern fish-processing operations.

other Atlantic provinces, UMF now embraces nearly all aspects of the seafishing business and, taken as a whole, ranks as one of the larger fishing industries in the region.

However, the biggest fishing firms in Nova Scotia today derive from somewhat different traditions: from the colourful offshore fishing heritage, particularly of Lunenburg; and from the large export firms of Halifax and other centres which once drew their fishing from the outports for shipment to overseas markets. The big firms also share business histories of successful mergers, acquisitions and expansions, as well as the rapid adoption of new technology, and an aggressive response to international markets.

National Sea Products Limited is one of the largest fish corporations in North America, and its main processing plant in Lunenburg is among the biggest in the world. Nova Scotia's second largest fishing firm is H. B. Nickerson and Sons Limited, whose Canso Seafoods plant is one of the most advanced on the continent. Both corporations have numerous branches and subsidiaries throughout Nova Scotia, and in Newfoundland and New Brunswick; as well as marketing and sales organizations in the United States and Canada.

Around 70 per cent of the groundfish taken by the fishermen of Atlantic Canada today is processed as fresh or frozen fillets. In Nova Scotia, the predecessors of National Sea pioneered the offshore banks in the fresh and frozen fish trade. While Lunenburg was still a major power in the traditional salt fish business, with 92 schooners on the banks, the salt-fish firm of W. C. Smith and Company in 1926 built cold storage facilities and turned to the fresh and frozen trade. The same year Lunenburg Sea Products sent its first three dory-fishing schooners to the banks in winter

A modern Nova Scotia fish processing plant.

to bring back iced groundfish. By 1934, twenty schooners were fresh-fishing on the banks and running their cargoes into Lunenburg, Lockeport and Halifax. One of the chief markets was Montreal where the fish was expressed in refrigerated cars on Canadian National Railways' old "Seafood Special".

With world salt fish markets in drastic decline in the 1920s and 1930s, both the inshore and schooner fishermen of Nova Scotia had bitterly opposed the introduction of trawlers. Though both trawlers and smaller fish draggers were in regular use in neighboring New England, the Canadian government in 1930 banned further development of the trawler fleet in this country. The 11 steam trawlers fishing from Nova Scotia ports in 1926 had dwindled to three by 1944, and in the fresh fish trade the dory-fishing schooners remained supreme on the Canadian Atlantic long after they were superseded in New England by the trawlers. The trawler ban probably set back the growth of our fishing technology temporarily, but it took place at a time when technical and industrial development was already restrained by a depressed economy. On the other hand, the ban probably did help in the survival of Nova Scotia's many important coastal communities.

The Nova Scotia schooners and the inshore fleet turned in record catches during the Second World War. But the trawlers had proven themselves to be the biggest and most reliable fish catchers. In Nova Scotia they were a necessity for large scale fish processing the year round. Yet the Canadian Government trawler policy relaxed only cautiously. Two wooden trawlers, *Cape North* and *Cape LaHave* had been built at Meteghan in the last years of the war, and by 1950 there still were only five trawlers fishing out of Nova Scotia ports.

Though United States fish imports directly after the war more than doubled and Canada supplied nearly 90 per cent of the import market, by 1951 competition particularly in frozen fish from Iceland, Norway and Newfoundland, had reduced the Canadian share to less than one third. Before Newfoundland joined Canada in 1949, the Canadian Atlantic fishery was predominantly that of Nova Scotia, augmented by the smaller gulf and inshore fisheries of New Brunswick, Prince Edward Island and Quebec. With Newfoundland and Labrador as a new province, Canada assumed responsibilities for a much larger deep sea fishery. Trawler policy changed the same year. Canadian shipyards lacked the technology to build steel fishing vessels at the time. Wooden trawlers were built at Smith and Rhuland in Lunenburg and other famed Nova Scotia yards, and the steel vessels imported. By 1962 Canada had 37 trawlers, and 28 of them were Nova Scotian.

However, it was a new federal policy in support of Canadian shipbuilding that had the most profound effect on the development of Nova Scotia's modern trawler fleets, and the large integrated fishing firms which depend upon them.

Subsidies to Canadian yards in the 1960s made them competitive with European builders, and they quickly acquired the technology of steel fishing vessel construction during the period when deep sea fishing fleets throughout the world were switching from traditional side-trawlers to the more efficient modern stern-trawlers. National Sea laid the basis for its present trawler fleet at that time, building 23 in the 1960s, and so far another nine in the 1970s. Of these all but four of the early vessels were built in eastern Canadian yards: 19 at Halifax Shipyards Ltd., five in Marystown, Newfoundland, two in Sorel, Quebec, and two at Ferguson Industries Ltd. in Pictou, Nova Scotia.

With their own deep-sea trawler fleets providing groundfish regularly 12 months of the year, the large integrated fishing firms are able to solve the fundamental problems of maintaining a constant supply of fish to their processing plants — provided, of course, there are enough fish to be caught. Co-ordinating trawler trips with the requirements of various plants helps maximize both catching and processing efficiency. Similarly integration, under a single or unified management, of all the specialized operations in sea fishing, from catching different species to primary processing and the manufacturing, marketing and sales of a wide variety of fish products and by-products, can maximize corporate performance and expand the company's share of international markets, as in other complex industries.

Indeed, the complexity of the fishing business, at the fish-catching and processing end, may make it appear as a collection of separate ''industries'' with little in common but the ocean itself. Between groundfishing and lobstering, or the herring business and the scallop industry, the differences often seem greater than the similarities. Each of these fisheries has its own federally administered rules, regulations and licenses concerning the usage of gear, boat sizes, fishing locations, species, conservation and quality control measures. Fishing techniques differ widely: trawlers, draggers and longliners take most of the groundfish; seiners fish the herring; offshore and inshore scallop draggers take scallops, and the ubiquitous, multi-purpose Cape-Island-type boats catch the inshore lobster in season and gill-net, longline, seine, drag or trap groundfish and other species during the rest of the working year. While the processing of groundfish and herring has similarities, scallops and lobsters, for example, require altogether different handling. However, the marketing processes are basically the same, though the individual fisheries remain relatively specialized. Thus, nearly every processor, large or small, regularly markets several different lines of seafood.

Hauling the trawl aboard a Nova Scotia stern trawler, with the cod-end containing a catch of 30,000 pounds.

Fisheries Diplomacy

It showed up first in the inshore fisheries of Nova Scotia and Newfoundland. Despite the new longliners and draggers built in the 1950s, inshore catches of groundfish on the Nova Scotia coast were relatively lower in the early 1960s. The cod were getting scarce. Fishermen blamed it on the big foreign fleets fishing as close as three miles offshore. The small fishing communities in Nova Scotia suffered, but not as much as in Newfoundland. In Canada's newest province the decision to build larger and longer-range inshore boats was coupled with the controversial closing of many isolated outports and efforts to consolidate the coastal populations in larger communities.

The rise of the huge fleets of factory trawlers, fishing the Northwest Atlantic off our coasts, was a post-war phenomenon made possible by new technology and the pressures on Europe to produce more food. Before the Second World War, the traditional fishing nations of Britain, France, Portugal, Spain and Norway worked the banks. Afterwards, they were joined by nations with modern fleets that had never fished in this part of the world before: Russia, Italy, East Germany, Poland, Denmark, Iceland and West Germany. By 1953, the British had produced the stern trawler *Fairtry,* a radical new factory freezer vessel which became a prototype for the new generation of east and west European deep sea trawlers of unsurpassed fishing power.

In the Northwest Atlantic the dramatic upsurge in modern trawler fishing began with the Russians in 1961. After scouting trips in 1954-56, the first Russian fishing unit of 52 large trawlers, four mother ships and two other support vessels arrived in 1961 from the Baltic. Taking 341 thousand metric tons, the U.S.S.R. outfished every other nation in the area that year, except Canada and the United

States. Within two years the Russian fishing fleet had grown to 250 ships on this coast, taking a third of their total catch in these waters between Georges Bank and Labrador. By 1971 they had surpassed Canada and the United States. As the Russian fishing effort expanded so did that of other nations. From 1,416 fishing vessels of all nations in 1962, the offshore fleets on this coast grew by 1974 to 2,057 vessels; and from a starting point of 500,000 registered tons in the late 1950s they had multiplied by 1974 to a total of 2,700,000 tons.

Catches, however, did not keep pace with the massive increases in vessel tonnage and fishing effort. The total catch for all countries fishing in the area had risen from 2,604,000 metric tons in 1962 to a high of 4,599,000 metric tons in 1968, then the figures began an inexorable decline. By 1974 the total catch was down to 4,047,000 metric tons, and in 1975 dropped to 3,808,000. Canada had doubled vessel tonnage from 1965 to 1974 and ended up catching 27 per cent less fish.

Severe over-fishing was depleting the stocks of the great Northwest Atlantic fishery. Historically, the idea was hard to grasp. This was the fishery that John Cabot had found so incredibly abundant; that John Smith believed was worth more than all the gold and silver of Spain; that for more than 400 hundred years had fed the rise and fall of empires and nursed the civilizations of Europe and America. According to the eminent Victorian biologist Thomas Huxley, our cod was inexhaustible, as indeed were all the great sea fisheries. Nothing man did could seriously affect the numbers of fish in the sea. The idea persisted into this century, and is still reflected in various views of the ocean as man's undiminishing storehouse. However, fisheries scientists had recognized the pressure on Northwest Atlantic fish stocks

Large Russian stern trawler on the offshore banks.

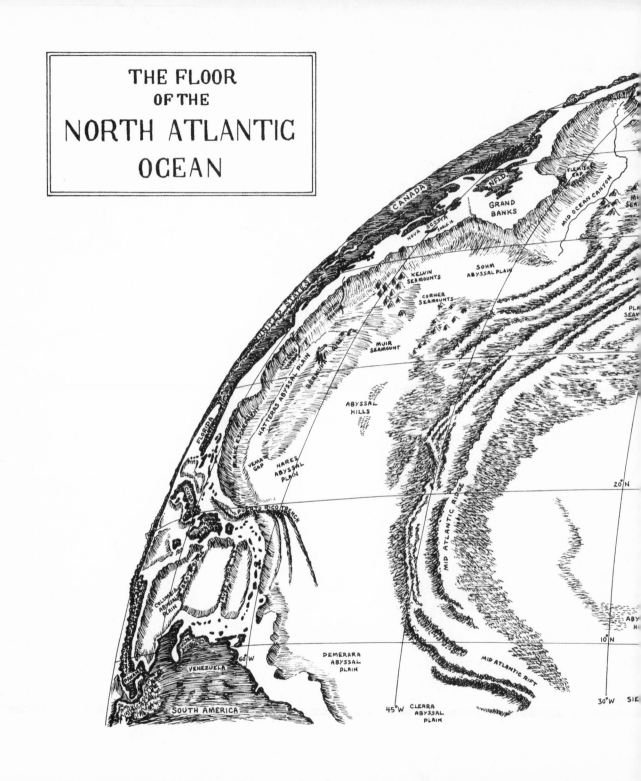

THE FLOOR
OF THE
NORTH ATLANTIC
OCEAN

This relief map of the floor of the Atlantic Ocean plainly shows the huge shelf off the coast of eastern Canada, running from Labrador south past Cape Cod. This shelf supports the famed fishing banks of the Northwest Atlantic, including Georges Bank off New England, the Nova Scotia Banks, and the Grand Banks of Newfoundland.

for some time. The problem was what to do about it.

The depletion of stocks of individual species in specific areas of the world's fisheries had occurred before. There had been depletion of the herring stocks on the Canadian Pacific coast, and in the 1940s indications of depletion of certain stocks off the New England coast. In fact, the signs of depletion off New England in 1949 led Washington to call the conference which established the International Commission for the Northwest Atlantic Fisheries. With a membership consisting of the nations participating in these fisheries, ICNAF was assigned the job of investigation, protection and conservation of the fishery resources in the Northwest Atlantic.

Though the fisheries were taking place within three miles of the Canadian and American coasts, it must be remembered that they were conducted in international waters over which neither Canada nor the United States had any special jurisdiction. The decisions and the work of ICNAF required the common consent of its international membership, and this made the application and enforcement of restraints on fishing difficult and only partially effective. ICNAF introduced gear regulations including allowable mesh sizes for trawls, and in 1972 adopted a quota system by which the total allowable catches of specific species in different zones of the fishery were annually calculated and apportioned among ICNAF members. Policing each fleet was the task of the nation concerned and thus largely voluntary. Scientists of all nations, sharing information on fish stocks and species within the international forum of ICNAF, helped identify the critical state of the fisheries.

Meanwhile, among western nations the climate of opinion concerning the physical environment was undergoing revolutionary changes. The sciences of ecology and oceanology were more firmly established. In Canada the Bedford Institute of Oceanography opened in 1969 in Dartmouth, Nova Scotia, followed by the development of Canada's first department of oceanography at Dalhousie University in Halifax. These and other marine research facilities have made this metropolitan area the largest ocean sciences centre on the Atlantic coast.

Public concern helped focus more research on the environment. Anxieties about the environmental impact of expanding industrial technology took the form of probes and protests against the pollution of air and water resources — including the oceans. While stringent anti-pollution and safety measures were applied to offshore oil exploration on the Nova Scotia shelf beginning in the 1960s, fears of major oil spills by tankers were justified. Canada's worst oil spill occurred in 1970 with the disaster of the tanker *Arrow* which went aground and broke up in Nova Scotia Chedabucto Bay, spewing its black cargo along the coast and killing marine and bird life in this historic sea fishing area.

The rising public interest in the fate of the oceans reflected recent and fundamental changes in our age-old ideas about them. From the days of the earliest sailors the oceans have been seen primarily as vast empty spaces, strange and dangerous, to be navigated with skill and fortitude. Today, those same oceans are perceived more as resources — great bodies of natural resources, renewable and non-renewable; subject to potential economic development, and to human abuse and even destruction as never before.

As modern technology opened up new possibilities for the exploitation of ocean resources, as in sea fishing and sea-bed mining, the traditional law of the sea became

outmoded. Guaranteeing freedom of the high seas, the international law formulated 300 years ago by the Dutch jurist Hugo Grotius to facilitate shipping, was inadequate to regulate the complex new usages of the ocean which were already underway. Beginning with a 1957 resolution to examine the law, the United Nations Law of the Sea conferences have taken 20 years to devise a draft treaty on the new international law of the sea, which still must be ratified by the 147 nations involved. Within these conferences completely new concepts were evolved and gradually accepted by the member nations. Most important to Canada was the consensus obtained on fisheries jurisdiction in the third Law of the Sea conference in 1975 making it possible for countries like Canada to adopt the 200-mile limit without provoking conflict.

However, Canada already had taken a series of initiatives over the years to protect our fisheries against the greatest concentration of foreign fishing power on the high seas. In 1958 and again in 1960 Canada's efforts in the Law of the Sea conference to gain agreement on extending our three-mile territorial limit to 12 miles were frustrated. To protect the inshore fisheries Canada unilaterally declared the 12-mile limit in 1964, followed in 1971 by the establishment of exclusive fishing rights for Canadians in the Bay of Fundy and Gulf of St. Lawrence on this coast. At the same time, agreements were reached with foreign nations traditionally fishing these waters to gradually phase out their fishing operations. Similar arrangements were made for Queen Charlotte Sound, Dixon Entrance and Hecate Strait on the Pacific coast.

Working within ICNAF in 1972, Canada attained recognition of the principle of preferential rights for coastal states, and in 1975 secured from ICNAF a 40 per cent

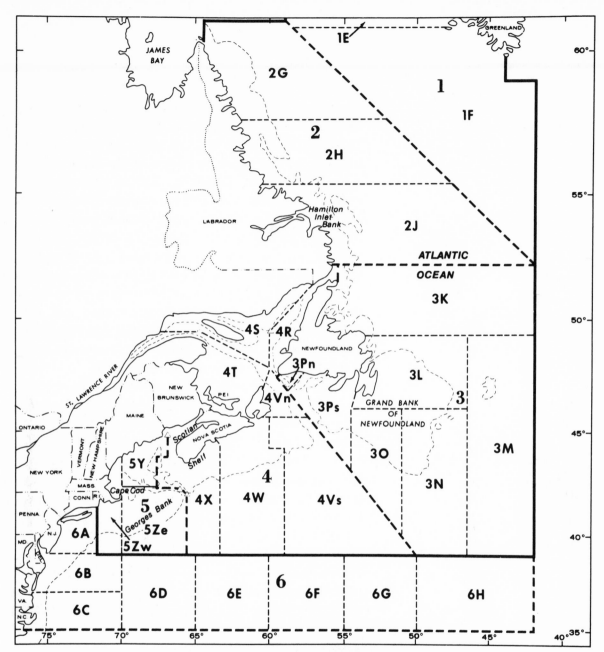

INTERNATIONAL COMMISSION
FOR THE
NORTHWEST ATLANTIC FISHERIES

Boundary of the Commission area. ——— Boundary of sub-areas............ ▬ ▬ ▬
Boundary of divisions............... — — — 100 fathom contour................. ∿ ∿

reduction in foreign fishing effort for groundfish, as well as a reduction in the total allowable catch.

This was the pattern of Canadian diplomatic initiatives leading to the consensus on the 200-mile limit in the third Law of the Sea conference. Basic to this consensus was the principle of optimum utilization, meaning that subject to conditions determined by Canada, other countries would have access to the fish which the Canadians declared surplus to their own requirements. This gave Canada effective control of the area without entirely excluding other countries, many of which over the centuries had enjoyed free access to the fishery in these waters.

Canadian fishing diplomacy was instrumental in promoting the compromise of optimum utilization at a time when the conference was deadlocked between coastal states refusing any obligation to foreign offshore fishermen, and the powerful distant-water fishing nations asserting historic rights. Canada had helped turn the 200-mile limit from the highly disputed proposition of the 1960s into one of practical acceptance. There was no fear of a Cod War such as Iceland endured with Britain in 1974 when the Icelanders extended their limit to 50 miles.

Before the Canadian 200-mile limit was declared on January 1, 1977 Canada had resolved with the U.S.S.R. the outstanding fishing problems that in 1975 had closed Canada's Atlantic ports to the Soviet fishing fleet, and within one year negotiated individual bilateral fishing agreements with the U.S.S.R., Poland, Portugal, Spain and Norway — the countries responsible for some 90 per cent of the foreign catch off our coasts.
Since January Canada also has signed an agreement with Cuba and, of course, already had a treaty with France.

The 200-mile limit gave Canada control of the fisheries

within 200 nautical miles of the Canadian coast, an immense actively-fished area of 502,000 square miles on the Atlantic, and 128,000 square miles on the Pacific coast. Such an extension of fisheries jurisdiction, from the existing 12-mile territorial limit, and including the Gulf of St. Lawrence and the Bay of Fundy, just about doubled the area of Canada's maritime responsibility. However, the 200-mile fisheries zone is not a territorial limit; nor is it the entire package debated in the Law of the Sea conference as an exclusive "economic zone" — only a part of it. The concept of the economic zone embraces seabed resources and shipping regulation as well as fisheries — a reason for its slow passage. Canada wants ratification of the new Law of the Sea treaty as soon as possible.

With declaration of the 200-mile limit, Canada in effect became owner and manager of all the fish stocks within the area. With full management rights, Canada had the right to determine the total allowable catch and the Canadian share, as well as declaring which stocks or species are surplus to Canadian needs; which nations may catch the surplus, when, and with what types of gear. It was a comprehensive answer to the question of what Canada could do about over-fishing and the dwindling fish stocks in the Northwest Atlantic. Within three months both the United States and the Soviet Union also declared 200-mile limits.

For the transitional year of 1977 Canada largely determined the conservation measures, the vessels permitted to fish, and the allocation of catches, on the basis of 1976 consultations and co-operation with ICNAF. The 200-mile limit leaves some 10 per cent of the fisheries off our coast, outside extended Canadian jurisdiction, including Flemish Cap and a part of the Grand Bank. International co-operation is required in administering these areas which are closely related to the 200-mile zone. Bilateral negotiations are underway with the United States concerning the borders of the Canadian and U.S. jurisdictions in the Gulf of Maine and on the Pacific coast, with France concerning the islands of St. Pierre and Miquelon, and with Denmark on the zone boundaries between Canada and Greenland in Davis Strait and Baffin Bay.

For Canada the 200-mile limit offers a vast new seaward frontier. The two major elements in conservation and control of the fisheries within this zone are scientific research and surveillance. Of the 502,000 square miles on this coast, however, only some 200,000 square miles covering the fishing banks require active air and sea patrols. This surveillance, carried out mainly by the Canadian Coast Guard with assistance from the Canadian Armed Forces and fisheries patrol vessels, is backed up with strong legal provisions and regulations governing the behaviour of foreign as well as Canadian fleets.

Every fishing vessel in the zone, foreign or Canadian, must be under Canadian licence, and every foreign fishing vessel must report on entering and leaving the 200-mile zone, as well as reporting regularly on catches and location. Detailed information on each foreign fishing vessel provided prior to licensing, plus its reports from the fishing zone are fed into a national computer network code-named Flash. Violators of Canadian regulations can lose the fishing vessel license, and captains may be fined up to $25,000. Furthermore, Canada's Minister of Fisheries and Environment has the power to cancel the licenses of an entire nation.

As the scientists see it, the basic task is to stabilize fish stocks in the zone and then rebuild them. Research is crucial. At least 60 stocks populate these waters and the

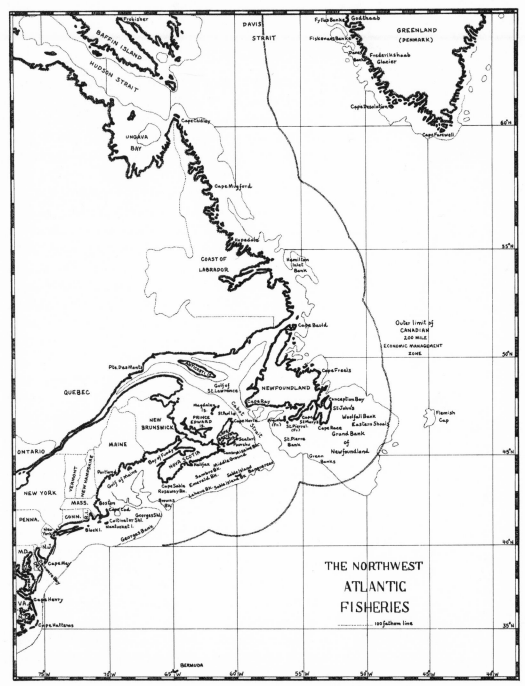

Boundary of the Canadian 200-mile fisheries zone.

scientists admit they simply don't know enough about them. If the necessary information had been available to them in the 1960s, depletion of the fish stocks and Canada's subsequent declaration of the 200-mile limit might not have occurred. Canada is now intensifying scientific research efforts, increasing fisheries research staff in the Atlantic region, and planning new research vessels.

The aim is to increase marine biological research and provide sound information that will take the traditional guesswork out of fisheries resource management. With a systematic approach in the Northwest Atlantic, Canadian scientists expect to be able to predict or at least detect early fluctuations and trends in plenty of time to adjust harvesting. Only with a strong capability to determine trends can they check problems, or give the fishing industry the necessary lead time for responding to opportunities as these develop. Scientific authorities expect to be able to provide this brand of advice on the fisheries within three or four years. Meanwhile Canada is taking a conservative approach in setting total allowable catch limits.

For this first year of the 200-mile limit, allowable catches for all nations were dropped 30 per cent to 668,500 metric tons, with foreign fleets absorbing nearly all the reduction, and doing their fishing in areas relatively distant from the major Canadian grounds. While the share of foreign nations dropped by 47 per cent and for some countries as much as 68 per cent, Canada's 1977 quotas rose slightly to 339,600 tons. And, though the allowable catch for all nations was cut, Canada's share of it rose from about one-third to over half.

With careful management of the 200-mile zone, Canadian fishermen's share of the catch is expected to rise steadily, though the total allowable catch in the zone must remain relatively low for some years in order to allow stocks to recover from the severe over-fishing of the 1960s and 1970s. There is no short-term solution to the problem of depleted stocks. In fact, Canadian scientists and fishermen are looking to the early 1980s for the potential restoration of the Northwest Atlantic fishery and the greater development of the Canadian fishing industry.

North West Atlantic Fishing Grounds —
Fishermen prepare their trawl net on a heaving deck